D0555695

In Character

JOHN MORTIMER

ALLEN LANE

ALLEN LANE
Penguin Books Ltd
536 King's Road
London SW10 0UH

First published 1983
Reprinted 1983 (twice)

ISBN 0 7139 15102

Set in VIP Plantin
Filmset, printed and bound in Great Britain by
Hazell Watson & Viney Ltd, Aylesbury, Bucks

British Library Cataloguing in Publication Data

Mortimer, John, *1923–*
In character.
1. Biography – 20th century
I. Title
920'.009'047 CT120

ISBN 0-7139-1510-2

Most of these interviews appeared in the *Sunday Times*, one in the *Daily Telegraph Magazine* and one in *Radio Times*. I am grateful to the editors of these papers, and to Brian MacArthur, Magnus Linklater and Don Berry at the *Sunday Times* who encouraged me to write them, and even undertook the daunting first step of telephoning the subjects.

Contents

Long Life – Short Sentences

LORD DENNING

SECTION ONE

(1) *What is Lord Denning?*

People often ask, 'What is Lord Denning?' 'Is he a power for progress and reform in the law?' Or, 'Is he fixed in the past, with the values of Rudyard Kipling, a patriotic subaltern at the start of the First World War?' 'Is he champion of the working man or the enemy of the unions?' 'Is he the most creative lawyer of our age, or a perverse judge with a strong streak of vanity?' Such are the questions people ask about Lord Denning.

Much light is thrown on the subject by his books. They deal with his life and his cases. Like his judgements, they are written in numbered paragraphs. Section Three.1.(1) of *The Family Story* is entitled 'Falling in Love'. It is two pages long and divided into sub-sections. Section Five.1.(4) is called 'The Things We Did', (i) 'Commuting to London'. Lord Denning often refers to himself as 'Tom'. He writes in short staccato sentences. His example in this is Sir George Jessel, a great Victorian Master of the Rolls. This style does not waste words. It is very infectious.

(2) *His accent and his charm*

For almost as long as many people can remember, Lord Denning has presided over the Court of Appeal. He was there every day until his recent retirement. His complexion was healthy. His eyes, as he himself has written, were kindly. His wig was ancient, not to say disintegrating. He spoke in the rustic tones of his native

Hampshire. Cynics say that this habit of speech is carefully preserved, like the French accent of the late Yvonne Arnaud. I do not accept this. He treated everyone with great courtesy. From the nervous young barrister to Miss Christine Keeler, whose life he investigated for the purposes of the Profumo Inquiry, everyone was reassured by his charm. No one can remember Lord Denning ill-tempered or impatient. His manner made appearing before him a great pleasure. His politeness helped the cause of justice.

SECTION TWO

(1) *I visit Lord Denning. He is 'out'*

It was a sunny Sunday evening in Lincoln's Inn. This haunt of lawyers was empty. Only a few children were playing on the lawn of the members' garden. I climbed to Lord Denning's flat and rang the bell. No answer. I climbed down again and found the Master of the Rolls standing up against a wall being photographed by Miss Sally Soames. This photographer was smiling. She was clearly overcome by his charm, which, at the age of eighty-one, is quite undimmed.

Later we sat together in his comfortable, rather untidy sitting room. On the walls were pictures painted by Lady Denning of their country house. A trout stream flows through their garden. Lord Denning walks with some difficulty now, but his eye is as bright as ever. We talked about my father and he said, 'I must be one of the few people around who remember him.'

Later he said, 'I must be one of the few people around who've sentenced anyone to death.'

(2) *The death penalty and natural justice*

'How did you feel about sentencing people to death?' I asked, 'Was it appalling?'

'Didn't worry me in the least. I did it lots of times. The jury had come to their decision, and it was the only sentence allowed for murder. I knew that if there were good reasons there'd be a reprieve.'

'You were in favour of the death penalty?'

'Once I was. For murder most foul. And I was reassured that Geoffrey Fisher, when he was Archbishop of Canterbury, agreed with me. But now I think it's wrong that we should ask society to do something, hang a man, that none of us would be prepared to do, or even watch. Times have changed.'

'But you believe in natural justice. I mean, you believe in a great abiding moral principle which is more important than the letter of the law?'

'I've always believed that, yes.'

'And that belief must be connected with your Christian faith.'

'Subconsciously, I'm sure it is,' Lord Denning said. 'It's the way I was brought up. There is a constant moral imperative. And it's only if it has a moral basis that the law can command respect.'

'So that the moral imperative, as you've just said, is constant and doesn't change with the times.'

'I think that's right.'

'So if the death penalty's unethical now, it must always have been unethical.' It was a rare opportunity, which I was unable to resist, to cross-examine Lord Denning. 'In fact, has the death penalty always been wrong but you didn't realize it at the time?'

'I think that must be so. Yes.' The witness made a clear admission, won the entire sympathy of the court, and left the cross-examiner speechless.

(3) *God as Master of the Rolls*

'Do you see judgement as part of the function of a Christian God? I mean, do you expect to be judged eventually?' I asked.

'On the Day of Judgement. I suppose so, yes. I haven't really got around to thinking about that yet.'

But I couldn't abandon the image of the Great Appeal Court, and the Almighty as Master of the Rolls.

'How do you think you'll get on in court?'

'Oh, I expect there'll be a few black marks against me.'

(4) *Home life, security, certainty and the First World War*
'Your childhood and home life were extremely happy and secure.'

'Absolutely secure. We never doubted the things we were taught to believe in.'

'And your mother was the driving force?' A fact true, I have noticed, of many extremely successful men.

'Mother was the strong one, yes.' Charles Denning was a dreamer and, Tom Denning says of his father, not a very good poet. He was a draper in the little town of Whitchurch in Hampshire, to which Lord Denning has returned to live. His father was a man who went to London no more than once or twice in his life, and yet so strong and secure was the family that of Charles Denning's sons Norman became an admiral, Reg a general and Tom a Law Lord and Master of the Rolls. Four of the boys fought in the First World War with great bravery and two died. Tom was fighting in the trenches at the age of eighteen. Jack, the eldest, who was killed in a useless and perhaps mistaken attack on the Somme, quoted Horace in his last letter home and said that it was sweet and honourable to die for your country.

'None of you had any doubts about the war?'

'None at all. As Reg said, the King and Parliament had decided on it. That was all we needed.'

'But later, after the appalling carnage, didn't a certain amount of disillusion set in?'

'I can't honestly say it did. We never questioned it, although, of course, the loss of life was a terrible thing. The best of the young men died.'

'You're a great questioner of authority in the law, but you didn't do so politically in the war, or afterwards in the Depression?'

'No. I don't think so. Let's say the law's my province, my special subject. I'm not a political animal.'

'You never thought of taking up politics?'

'Only once. There was a seat going before the 1945 election. It was the time when Hartley Shawcross got into Parliament for Labour. I might have done something about it, but of course I became a judge in 1944 and that put me out of it.'

'Would you have stood for Labour or the Conservatives?'

'Oh, I hadn't got around to thinking about *that*.'

(5) *Not conservative with a small 'c'*

'Forget about politics then. Are you conservative with a small "c" or liberal with a little "l"?'

'Oh, I'm not conservative. People have said the Court of Appeal's very conservative, they forget that when Donaldson put the three dockers in prison in the Industrial Court we let them out. Well, we'd been told there was the danger of a general strike. Most lawyers are conservative. That's what's wrong with them. They seem to have a vested interest in not changing the law. I would have to say that I'm on the liberal, or the progressive side. I believe in equal opportunity for everybody, and as an old grammar-school boy, I believe in independent schools. I believe in an élite of excellence, certainly not in an élite of the upper class. I would be against that.'

'You've tried to move the law forward, to make it more fair and reasonable?'

'I've tried to, yes. People say that moving the law forward should be left to Parliament, and not to the judges. Of course, when you look at some of the judges, they may be right.'

'And you've always tried to do justice in the case before you, in spite of precedents.'

'That's always my rule. To do justice in the instant case. The House of Lords doesn't agree with that.' The running battle between the Master of the Rolls and the Law Lords is a legal spectacular which will, in the years to come, be sorely missed. Whatever anyone thinks of Lord Denning, his absence will make the law a lot less fun. 'They think the great aim is certainty in the law. My aim is justice. If I don't feel I've done justice in a case I can't sleep at nights.

'You see, there are always two ways of interpreting a statute,' Lord Denning went on. 'Words are never absolutely clear. And when there's a choice I always tend to the interpretation which will do justice. I'm not sure the House of Lords always thinks that way.'

Lord Justice Russell once accused Lord Denning of being a 'Bassanio man', for in the trial scene in *The Merchant of Venice* Bassanio pleads to the judge:

> And I beseech you,
> Wrest once the law to your authority:
> To do a great right, do a little wrong.

But Lord Denning has protested that it was Portia who found a way of interpreting the Venetian law of contract which did justice, defeated Shylock and saved Antonio's flesh. Lord Denning says that he is a Portia man himself.

'You weren't entirely happy when you were in the Lords?'

'No. The dominating factor there was Lord Simmons and we two never saw exactly eye to eye. I've been much happier back in the Court of Appeal.'

(6) *Sans peur et sans rapproche*

'You started as a divorce judge and you've said that no one who's been divorced should sit as a judge in that division.'

'Once no one could. In the old days it was like being invited to the Queen's Enclosure at Ascot. Now I don't think inquiries are even made.'

'Don't you believe that people who've made mistakes in their lives can come to fair decisions?'

'I'm sure they can. The problem arises when the public gets to know about it. Then they might say, "The judge was on my husband's side because he'd been divorced too." I think it's all right if people don't know. But really a judge should be *sans peur et sans rapproche*.'

'And you may have a lot of erring, fallible human beings on juries. I mean, you *are* in favour of the jury system?' I asked.

'Of course. I agree with Patrick Devlin. "Trial by jury is the lamp that shows that freedom lives." It's how a jury should be selected that's the problem. It used to be said that juries were entirely composed of middle-aged, middle-class men. That was true, but they came to some very reliable decisions. Now the age has been reduced to eighteen, and there's no "householder" qualification.'

'But surely you're meant to be tried by your peers?'

'By your peers, yes. Not by every crook and swindler in the neighbourhood.'

'You talk about middle-aged men. Surely you don't object to women on juries . . .?'

'Certainly not. I've always been in favour of the emancipation of women. In divorce I made the decisions about a deserted wife's right to the matrimonial home.'

'Do you think the law's swung too far now, in favour of divorced wives?'

'Now they can get jobs. Yes. It may have swung too far.'

'Can I ask you about the criminal law? What do you think about our appalling prison conditions? And does prison do anyone any good?'

'If you ask me that, I can't say prison does any good. When I was a judge I went round and found the closed prisons very bad, and now they're even more overcrowded. But what can you do? Society demands a penalty, and I agree with that.'

'Do you think anyone will invent a more creative alternative to prison?'

'In the old days we sent them to Sydney and they did very well. I don't think that was a harsh punishment. Admittedly the journey out was bad.'

(7) *His great achievements*

I asked Lord Denning what he considered his great achievements in the law.

'People always ask that. I think of the *High Trees* case and the other cases which decided that a promise intended to be binding, and intended to be acted on, could be enforced in law. I think of the whole body of administrative law we built up to control bureaucracy and the powers of ministers and local government. And we had the cases which prevent international companies running off with the assets. I've always been keen on protecting the City of London as Lord Mansfield [the great eighteenth-century Chief Justice, another of Lord Denning's heroes] was. I think we've done more to improve the law in the last thirty years than was done in the fifty years before that.'

'Do you see your attitude to the law dying out as you retire?'

'I have great hope for the young. Students always receive me so warmly. I hope they will carry it on.'

'But then bright young students grow into conventional old judges, when they're dressed with a little brief authority.'

'Yes.' Lord Denning looked quite sad for a moment. 'I think it may be so.'

(8) *Fair's fare?*

'In the GLC case about London Transport we had to consider the fairness to the rate-payers of Bromley. I mean, why should they pay a lot more rates so that other people could travel more cheaply? And, of course, the statute said that London Transport had to pay its way.'

'But you have said principles of justice can be more important than purely legal considerations. Hadn't the London electors voted in Mr Livingstone and his subsidized fares policy? Shouldn't the principle of democracy have been applied?'

Lord Denning shook his head and, in this instance, took a more legalistic view.

'The words of the statute,' he said, 'were quite clear in that case.'

I suppose the difficulty with natural justice is that you can never be quite sure of its source. Does it come from God, or the GLC electorate, or the rate-payers of Bromley?

(9) *The intention to defame*

'The law of libel is in a most terrible mess,' said Lord Denning, and anyone who has had to deal with that highly philosophical and obscure branch of the law would surely agree. 'All sorts of committees have reported but no one does anything about it.'

'What sort of libel law would you have?'

'It should depend on a real intention to defame, and not the mere fact that someone is defamed. The fact shouldn't be so important as the intention. I'd like to see judges with the power to sit without juries. Juries hate newspapers.'

'Do you think our present libel laws are a danger to free speech?'

'Yes. I think in a way they are.'

SECTION THREE

The changes in his time. 'What is Lord Denning?'

'Of course, I've seen society change,' Lord Denning said. 'Sexual standards have gone completely. I suppose it may be the pill and all that. And standards of honesty have declined. In the old days no one ever suggested the police were lying, or corrupt. Now they're cross-examined about it in every case.'

'Do you think that's just because cross-examiners have become bolder, not because the police weren't always fallible?'

'No. I think the old force was smaller, and was, in fact, honest. But now there's corruption in so many things, local government, building contracts – you know, a back-hander to the foreman to say the foundations are laid properly. On the other hand, yes, I think we have become more humane. And judges are less alarming.'

'But the law's become ruinously expensive.'

'You're all right if you're a big company, or if you've got legal aid. If you're in the middle it's impossibly expensive. I think legal aid should be extended. And I think if you're sued by a litigant with legal aid and you win, the state should pay your costs. After all, it paid the man to sue you.'

'Have you found it difficult to make decisions, as a judge?'

'It's not nearly as anxious as being at the bar. If you're an advocate you want your client to win, you want to do well for him, and for your career and so on. When you're a judge you don't care who wins exactly. All you're concerned with is justice. As I told you, unless I feel that I've done justice I can't sleep easily at night.'

*

Lord Denning gives the impression of being a man of great serenity. The home he was brought up in gave him security, his faith has given him clear direction, his love of England, the countryside he lives in, and his life with his second wife after the tragic death of his first, clearly bring him great happiness. He looks forward to speaking in the House of Lords, and keeping extremely busy in the years to come.

And yet, for all his serenity, Tom Denning's is a character of some contradictions. He is a liberal and a progressive whose views on sex are not far removed from those of Mrs Whitehouse, a valiant defender of democracy who has roused the anger of the Left, a defender of juries who seems to want to confine judgement by your peers to a certain age and type of peer. Of course, he has seen a great deal of life, but he has been a judge for nearly forty years and a very successful barrister before that, and his view has always been formed on the well-protected side of the courtroom. It may be that he finds it hard to think of life as lived by those without his great advantage of a happy family life and a secure faith. It may indeed be that a book could be written about Lord Denning as a far more complex character, in which all these seeming contradictions might be resolved; but such a book could not be expressed in such clear and simple terms. It would require, of course, far longer sentences.

The Interrogation Chansonette

GEORGES SIMENON

'You've said there's no such thing as a criminal.'

'Criminologists agree. Professor Sydney Smith of Edinburgh said: "Criminals are ordinary people like you and me." '

'You believe that?'

'Down the lake here, at Vevey, two old men, men in their seventies, had a quarrel in a café . . . about the weather, politics, nothing at all. And one hit the other on the head with a glass. Killed him. He looked at his old friend in horror. "Jean," he said, "what have I done to you?" Is that a criminal? I don't believe in culpability.'

'Could *you* murder someone?'

'I don't know. I hope not, but who knows?'

Georges Simenon, seventy-nine years old, with a full head of grey hair, neat cotton trousers, a white shirt and a bow of red string as a tie, which made him look like a judge in some old movie set in the Deep South, smiled almost wistfully. Outside the window a little pale Swiss sunshine fought its way through the rain. In his patch of garden a cloud of birds settled to eat the huge quantity of grain he puts out for them, and a plump cat watched them eagerly from behind the two-hundred-year old cedar tree.

'But doesn't your hero, Inspector Maigret, spend his time bringing people to justice?'

'Maigret wants to find out the truth. Quite often when he has found it he lets the criminal go. Or he hands him to the court for judgement. Maigret doesn't make judgements, and he detests the court. In your country the courts are even more absurd than in

France. Don't you still sit there wearing the perruque in order to hang people?'

I confirmed that the perruque lives on in British justice but not, at least for the moment, hanging.

'The death penalty! I have been so much opposed to that all my life! In France lawyers had to attend the executions. I never found one French lawyer who was in favour of the guillotine. Never one!'

'Maigret may not like the court, but isn't he the voice of conscience? He always reminds one of the Police Chief in *Crime and Punishment*, the understanding old uncle that the criminal has to trust.'

'Let me tell you this. Maigret is founded on a number of policemen I knew well. Good policemen, in Liège, also in Paris. Maigret is the master of the interrogation *chansonette*.'

'How does that go?'

'The *chansonette*? It is the police questioning like a little song. Shall I show you?'

'Please do.'

'The suspect is brought in and the inspector smiles at him, so gently, and he says: "I can't think why you're here. It must be some mistake. I mean, *you* can't be guilty of anything, can you? I mean, I've got nothing against you written down here. Can *you* imagine why you've been brought to me?"

' "I suppose it might be something to do with that business at the Café du Lac last night." The prisoner tries to be helpful, he is lulled by the *chansonette* like a baby.

' "The Café du Lac? Was there anything there last night? Oh yes, I seem to remember some little trouble. You didn't have anything to do with *that*, did you?"

' "Well, it's only that I'd called in for a drink and . . ."

' "Of course you were there. No harm in that at all." The inspector yawns as if he's very bored and smiles: "Well, I suppose now you've taken all the trouble of coming in to see me I might as well ask you what you were doing."

'After an hour or two of this the prisoner does, what do you call it, *everything* in his trousers out of fear and confesses everything too. We call it the *chansonette*, the little lullaby.'

I do not know if Simenon would ever have made a criminal. He might have been a peculiarly lethal Inspector of Police.

Simenon's parents were *petit bourgeois*, what he calls 'the little people', a race of unsung, simple and decent heroes whom he regards, at times, with the sentimental eye of his late neighbour in Switzerland, Charlie Chaplin, a 'little man' who had managed to become a millionaire. Simenon's father was an insurance salesman, a good Catholic, and contented with his lot. His mother, anxious, highly strung, terrified of poverty, conferred on the young Georges the inestimable advantage of taking in lodgers, a number of young Polish and Russian students from Liège University.

'They taught me to read, those students. By the time I was twelve I'd read Gogol and Dostoyevsky. Then I read Chekhov. I have always loved Chekhov above everything. Later I read Conrad.'

'Were you religious?'

'Oh, very religious. When I was eleven I got a scholarship to the College of Saint Louis and I was thinking of becoming a priest. I got rid of that idea when I was thirteen.'

'What happened when you were thirteen?'

'I made love for the first time. I saw all that about guilt and sin was nonsense. I found out that all the sins I'd heard about were not sins at all!'

After a lifetime in which the number of his novels and love affairs has reached epic, almost mythical proportions, M. Simenon, once destined for the priesthood, one-time police reporter, former social secretary to the Marquis de Tracy, sat in his small, neat room with a few books, a large TV set on a chromium stand, a small white desk and a divan bed spread with a fur rug. His five cars have been sold. His twenty-four Buffets, his Picassos, his Légers, his Soutine and his numerous Vlamincks are in store, nothing hangs on the wall but what looks like a paper calendar from the local grocer's. He hasn't written a novel since he moved out of his huge mansion, away from his eleven servants, his three secretaries and his chef in a tall white hat, to live with his second wife's Italian maid, Teresa, who is a middle-aged, comfortable lady of the kind who might be seen presiding with great charm and authority over some Italian pensione. She sat with us as we talked and smiled with joyful anticipation as Simenon embarked on the story of what happened when he climbed a tree at the age of thirteen.

'She was three years older than I. We were on holiday in a little village near Liège. I was just a boy, you understand? I was wearing short pants. And she asked me to get some berries for her. She thought them pretty. When I came down the tree my legs were bleeding and she licked the blood off them. Then she was on top of me. We made love.'

'Something you have done with many women since then.'

'Oh yes!' Teresa smiled with undisguised pride and spoke in French. 'M. Simenon has done so with many, many women.'

Since he stopped writing novels Simenon has published his *Mémoires Intimes*, a book which reveals a sexual history as dedicated, hard working and almost as exhausting to contemplate as his prodigious literary achievement. After twenty years of marriage his first wife Tigy, an artist, discovered that he was having an affair with their housekeeper Boule, a lady who would wade out 'with the water up to her breasts' to give the tireless author his breakfast as he sat typing on his boat. Simenon confessed to adultery, not only with Boule but with hundreds of women, including a steady daily procession of prostitutes.

After the war Simenon moved to Canada where he fell in love with his French-Canadian secretary Denise, known in his writings as 'D'. For a while he was able to live in some harmony with Tigy, Boule and 'D'. Things seem to have gone fairly smoothly until 'D' became pregnant with Simenon's daughter Marie-Jo and Tigy left. After Simenon and 'D' were married he continued to visit brothels and she, he has written, accompanied him and advised him on the choice of girls.

In an earlier work, *When I Was Old*, Simenon has described how he had paid with a silver watch his dying father had given him in order to enjoy, at the age of sixteen, the favours of a negress, a prostitute in Liège (he had to lie to his mother and report the watch as lost to the police in order to account for its disappearance). He has also described the day he made love to four prostitutes in rapid succession during the time it took his wife to pack for a visit to New York.

'But why prostitutes?'

I remembered the answer to my question in his book: 'The more ordinary the woman is,' Simenon had written, 'the more one can consider her as "woman", the more the act takes on significance.'

'Look at this.' He crossed the room now and, from somewhere near the huge, silent television, snatched up a magazine. On the cover a naked model, pouting at the camera, was fighting a losing battle with a silk sheet. The seventy-nine-year-old writer's hand was shaking with indignation. 'Look! This is not a "woman". This is a sophisticated doll! A toy!' He dropped the magazine as though it might carry an infection. 'I tell you, I have found many real "women" among prostitutes. I treated them with consideration and like a gentleman. I always let them have their pleasure first. And of course I was enough of a connoisseur to know if their pleasure was faked.'

I thought of Lausanne, the town in which Simenon now lives. I remembered the clean streets, the cathedral, the inviting chocolate shops, the children roller skating in perfect silence, the middle-aged citizens padding about in their fur-lined zipped-up boots, trilby hats and excellent suede jackets. Did the almost octogenarian novelist sally forth each day to some obscure red light district of which I was unaware? I hesitated over the question, but Teresa's smile didn't alter when I asked it.

'Do you still . . .?'

'Oh no.' Simenon looked at his present companion with considerable affection. 'Now I have found a true "woman", that is no longer necessary, I assure you.'

'And would you mind,' I asked Teresa, 'if while you were packing for a trip M'sieur Simenon called in four prostitutes?'

'Not at all.' Teresa's smile was imperturbable. '*Je ne suis pas jalouse*. M'sieur Simenon must do as he likes, of course. He is a free spirit, *un esprit libre*.'

They were both smiling, beaming at me, quite contented, the Darby and Joan of the permissive society.

'You will drink something? What will you drink?'

Doing my best to enter into the spirit of Maigret and the Brasserie Dauphin I thought I'd have a beer.

'Very well,' said Simenon, 'and when your wife arrives to collect you we will have a little *coup de champagne*. You know, I have always drunk a lot. In Paris my lowest consumption of wine was three bottles of St Émilion a day. And it was only when I moved to America that I began to feel like an alcoholic.'

'You are not whom I thought you would be,' Simenon had said when we first met. 'You are not that M'sieur Mortimer from the *Sunday Times* who was a highbrow and a friend of André Gide.'

'No,' I confessed. He was thinking, no doubt, of the late, greatly lamented Raymond Mortimer.

'You are not a highbrow?'

'Not at all.'

'Neither am I. I knew Picasso well. He was not at all intelligent. In fact he had no culture. He painted on an impulse. Gide was a highbrow and a homosexual. I think it made him very unhappy. He wrote how much he admired my books. Personally I found his unreadable, but I never told him that.'

'What do you read?'

'I read the Penal Code and the Bible. The Bible is a cruel book. Perhaps the cruellest book ever written.'

'What crime writers?'

'Dashiell Hammett I like very much. As he did, I used to write so many stories for . . . what do you call them?'

'Pulp magazines.'

'Yes. I used to write stories set in America and Africa. I got all the information out of encyclopaedias. And when I earned enough money to go to such places they were never as beautiful as the way I had described them . . .'

'Sherlock Holmes?'

'Too mechanical.'

Mechanical! I blinked as at some blasphemy, but then I supposed it was understandable. Faced with the eager arrival of four prostitutes in a morning, Holmes would have fled in terror, no doubt, to the private world of the hypodermic syringe and the violin.

'I write about small people, simple people. I write about the naked man in society. Great men do not interest me. Napoleon I detest. You know, after he'd lost the lives of 30,000 men in some battle Napoleon wrote to Josephine and said, 'It'll count for nothing tomorrow when I'm in your arms.'

'When did you first write "Maigret"?'

'I was twenty-five – and he was forty-five. I sent three novels to my publisher, Fayard. He was a big man and he looked at me and said, "It's no good. These stories have no mathematical problems, no love story, no good and bad characters and no happy endings!" And then he gave me a contract for eighteen novels. Since I thought of Maigret I have never been poor. I think I have written seventy-two Maigret novels altogether.'

'Seventy-nine,' Teresa corrected him.

'Ah yes. You see, she knows everything about me.'

Simenon's methods of writing are well known. He would make sure that there was no illness in his household and no other problem to disturb his concentration. He would then retreat into his room with an array of pipes and sharpened pencils and write at an extraordinary speed. Three quarters of the Maigret novels were written in seven days. After a couple of days' revision, each book was sent off. He never looked at it again.

'I gave up writing novels in February 1972. Since then I have lived very simply in this small house. I have an office in the town, and secretaries there. They deal with all the business . . .'

'Why did you give up?'

'I was getting too old. It's very tiring to get into the skin of a character. Very tiring. That is why I had to write fast. Seven days was quite long enough to be in someone else's skin, it was so painful I had to get it over. Now I'm happy to be in my own skin all the time.'

'But you've written your *Mémoires Intimes*. Why did you decide to do that?'

'Because of Marie-Jo. She always wanted her name on one of my books. You know her name is on the cover of the *Mémoires*.'

At the age of eight, Simenon's daughter insisted that he gave her a wedding ring. She committed suicide when she was twenty-five and asked to be cremated with the ring on her finger. One of her letters, printed at the end of his long autobiographical account of writing, travelling, bringing up children and love affairs, begins in English: 'You Daddy, my "Lord and Father".' One of her last ended: 'I'm lost in the space, the silence of the death. Forget my tears but please, believe in my smile, when I was your little girl, so many years ago.'

'But why did you tell so much about yourself?'

'Everyone else was writing about me. I thought it was time to tell the truth.'

My wife came to fetch me and Simenon stood gallantly, kissed the tips of her fingers and poured us all *un petit coup de champagne*. He told her that women were more intuitive than men. And then it was time to go.

'I enjoyed our talk,' said the old writer, back in his own skin after so many years of unremitting labour. 'But you see my English is not so good. I'm not used to it.'

'You speak it very well.'

'It's true.' Simenon was thoughtful. 'I dream in English very often. I wonder why that is.'

When we went out it was raining again on the big cedar tree and on the garden where the ashes of Marie-Jo, a child who seems to have loved her father too much, are scattered. It was raining on the cloud of birds that Simenon keeps fed so generously, and on the sleek cat that watches them all the time.

No Comment from On High

ARCHBISHOP RUNCIE

Easter week, 1982. As the lights of freedom are extinguished in Eastern Europe, as women and children face execution in Iran, as the queues of hopelessly unemployed school-leavers lengthen, as world-destroying armaments proliferate like houseflies and the British Navy sails off to shed blood on some distant island, the time seems, to the roving interviewer, appropriate to put a few searching questions to God. The Almighty moves, as is well known, in a mysterious way, but it would be comforting to know what immediate plans He has for our future. Has He wearied of His creation? Is He relying on His mysterious gift of free will to put an end to all our problems? Has He at least an Easter message which will help us understand His darker purposes?

He is not, of course, available for interviews, which is why I drove through the gates of Lambeth Palace one warm spring evening and walked across the quadrangle, where the cherry trees were blooming round the statues of angels, to put my questions to God's surrogate, or junior officer, Dr Robert Runcie, Primate of All England, Archbishop of Canterbury, and head of the world-wide Anglican Communion.

'I want to know about God. I mean, is He a personal God?'

'He can't be *less* than personal.'

'Very well, so He is personal.'

I was sitting on one of Dr Runcie's sofas in the living-room of his flat at the top of the palace. Dr Runcie, who looks thin, suntanned and in good condition at the age of sixty, was elegant in a black suit and purple waistcoat. He had invited me to join him in a Campari and soda, and had reminded me of the distant time when we both had rooms in Meadow Buildings, at Christ Church, Oxford. He had greeted me with a warm handshake, and instant hospitality, but I was off in pursuit of a more enigmatic character who had never, so far as I knew, had rooms in Meadow Buildings.

'So He's a personal God who can do what He wants with His universe. He's omnipotent?'

Dr Runcie immediately got the drift of an old argument and played a defensive stroke.

'So you're going to ask me about children with leukaemia,' he said. 'I can't be lured into that.'

'Children with leukaemia and concentration camps. Why did an omnipotent God allow the murder of eight million Jews?'

It's the question I have long wanted to put to God, but Dr Runcie, with the best will in the world, was unable to help me.

'I'm an agnostic on that. I don't know God's reason. I do believe that there's no human tragedy so great that it can't be redeemed in Christ.'

'But what does being redeemed in Christ mean if you're a Jew about to be gassed?'

'As I said, I'm an agnostic about God's purpose. But I believe we're responsible for the mess we make of His creation. That's the story of the cross . . .'

'Isn't the story of the cross a harsh story? I mean, as a father, can you imagine having your son killed for whatever reason?'

'The story of the crucifixion shows us how God as Christ enters into human suffering, and takes part in it.'

'But what was God's motive in creating human suffering, and the suffering of the crucifixion?'

'As I say, I'm an agnostic about that.'

At which moment, the archbishop's chaplain came in and asked for two minutes about the Falkland Islands where the inhabitants are, it seems, loyal members of the Church of England who had been raided by a Catholic junta.

'I'm sorry to interrupt you,' Dr Runcie said, 'just when we were deeply into the problem of evil . . .'

The archbishop was back, the Campari was replenished, and the conversation resumed. I started with an unexpected similarity between my own life and that of the Primate of All England.

'I was fascinated to discover that you also had a blind father you read to. What did you read?'

'Oh, the racing pages. And endless articles by J. L. Garvin in the *Observer*. That was a kind of verbal Bovril. My father was a working man who did very well. He became an electrical engineer for Tate & Lyle in Liverpool, which is where I was born.'

'Did you mistake him for God?' I asked. 'I've been accused of mistaking my father for God.'

'I suppose Freud would have told me that. My father was a good man, but he thought I spent far too much time in church.'

'Was your mother religious?'

'She was a very sentimental reader of detective stories. She loved going to the cinema, Edgar Wallace, God and the British Empire. She made us all stand up when the King spoke on the wireless at Christmas.'

'So how did you first meet God?' I was beginning to feel uneasily that Dr Runcie might not have had such a long, or close, association with the Almighty as I had been led to believe.

'I had an older sister. I was much the youngest of the family, sort of autumn leaf. She took me to a service at St Faith's in Crosby. I don't know who St Faith was, some virgin who was martyred during the reign of the Emperor Diocletian, and I remember being very impressed. Then the Church got hold of me. I became an altar boy which appealed to the theatrical side of my nature. I was set to running the boys' club, and I played the black wise man in the nativity play. I think I'm the only person who was actually converted at his own confirmation service. But most of my friends were ungodly.'

'I was at Oxford in the heyday of Freddie Ayer, and "Language, Truth and Logic". It was quite hard to hold on to belief and I had many conflicts. Graham Greene said of someone he was not so much a character in conflict as a person in a state of civil war. I think I'm like that. Faith is a great gift which can bring peace to the war within you. God is a great mystery to live by. But I still find a lot of trenchant truth in all sorts of people. Even people like you, of course.' For a moment Dr Runcie, who had been consistently cheerful during our conversation, looked almost depressed. 'When one is an archbishop of Canterbury, one has to rally the troops. But I can't think of Jesus as a "pal". That just seems to diminish the mystery.'

'But this mystery, which you can't explain . . . what does it do for you?'

'I'll tell you. I used to go for walks with E. M. Forster. And he said he couldn't take to religion because it was all about sin. And I said: "Then why do you go to chapel at King's?" and Forster said: "Because it makes you feel a bit small. It makes you go down on your knees." '

'I can understand that. I can understand the importance of feeling your own insignificant place in the universe, but to get back to God . . .'

'Yes,' Dr Runcie smiled, waiting tolerantly in the face of my religious insistence.

'Would you like Him, do you think, if you were really to know all about Him?'

'Jeremiah shook his fist at God and asked Him what He was about. I don't believe prayer is necessarily peaceful. It may mean arguing with God.'

I began to feel a little more secure and at one with Dr Runcie and the Prophet Jeremiah, at least in an occasional desire to ask God a few awkward questions.

'And this God you argue with, what's He like exactly?'

'He's not an amiable father like me. He makes demands.'

'Is He a judge?'

'No.'

'But you believe in an after-life?'

'Of course. I can't believe, when I see the promise of Christ expressed in a particular person, that that's all coming to an end. But as for the geography and climate of the after-life . . . well, I'm an agnostic about that too.'

'So you don't see God as a celestial Lord Chief Justice?'

'Not at all. I had an old landlady when we were at Oxford. And when we got into any sort of trouble, she'd say: "There's one above who seeth all." I can't think of God like that.'

'But this Easter, if you had to give a message about God to a bunch of unemployed school-leavers waiting in a dole queue in north-east England, what would you say?'

'I'm a bit suspicious of messages from archbishops' palaces boomed out to dole queues, but I suppose I'd say that no human situation is so tragic that it can't be turned to good effect. I'd say that there's a future that's worth waiting for.'

'You mean a future on earth?'

'Oh yes. And that, despite all appearances, the world is on our side. If we were more Christian, we'd be more concerned with human values than regulating the money supply or curing inflation. We've produced a competitive society which condemns anyone who doesn't succeed on its own terms. It's very cruel, and it's a new form of deprivation.'

They were the words of a good man who is genuinely distressed by the politics of the market place. For a moment, there was a rift in the clouds, and God could be seen smiling. I stifled the unworthy suspicion that He had, in a rare and benign moment, joined the Fabian Society or at least become a Tory wet.

And then we were away to new topics, to war, because Dr Runcie is the first Archbishop of Canterbury to have fought in battle since the Middle Ages, and violent death.

He said: 'I have interviews with anti-blood sports campaigners, and when they say: "Have you ever killed an animal?" I say, "No, I've only killed people." '

'Tell me about it.' I knew that the twenty-year-old Runcie, with a father who brought him up on Burns and Harry Lauder, had left Oxford to become a lieutenant in the Scots Guards.

'There were two things. The first was when I'd been very successful in knocking out a German tank. I went up to it and saw four young men dead. I felt a bit sick. Well, I was sick, actually.

'The other time was when a German tank was shelling our

position, and a very eager little man in specs came up to me and he said: "Shall I go and discover where that tank is?" Well, I knew it would be a good thing to find out, and also thought that if he went, he might be killed. Anyway I said: "Yes, why don't you go?" And I saw him shamble off in a very unsoldierly way in his baggy trousers. Half an hour later, he was dead. I won't say that incident led directly to my becoming a priest, but it had a lot to do with it. I thought, "I'll make up for that some day." '

'What do you think of military padres?'

'All that glib patriotic stuff is difficult for me. But of course as an archbishop I have to live with it. I can do a good Armistice Day sermon at a public school, just as I can do a good middle-class confirmation.'

'But you're for nuclear disarmament?'

'For all sorts of disarmament. We haven't had a nuclear war yet, but we've had terrible misery caused by the arms trade making a fortune out of small wars. I'm in touch with East European churches about disarmament. Of course, I don't know if they're all just tools of the Kremlin. But we must try, and we must keep on trying.'

'One thing that worries me about God.'

'*One* thing?'

'I mean, is He just ours? You have said that if you had happened to have been born in Delhi, you'd probably be a Hindu, or in Iran a Muslim.'

'Oh yes. I can't believe in a God who only saves people who live in certain latitudes. I used to lecture to Hellenic cruises about mosques, and I found great spiritual value in them. They are so light and airy, and domestic with carpets, and no real hierarchy, and one day a bunch of Christians marched into a mosque and sang a "Gloria", and the very religious Mohammaden woman in charge of the tour looked at me sadly and said: "You see what we're up against?" I must say I had some sympathy with her.'

'So does it matter which religion we have?'

'I find the easiest way to enlightenment is through Jesus Christ. I find the greatest fulfilment in Him. But I don't believe in creating a vacuum into which we insert the Christian religion. I went to

Rangoon and found a Buddhist priest examining some teenagers. One of the questions was: "What ethical effect does a belief in the after-life have on our actions?" I thought that was very good. I'm against extravagant claims made for one faith, but of course, as an archbishop, it doesn't do to let the side down.'

'Which brings us to the Pope . . .'

On a recent visit to Liverpool Cathedral, Dr Runcie had been shouted at and booed by a section of alleged Christians, Protestants who wished to protest against his meeting with the Pope.

'I was sorry about that business in Liverpool. I can understand strong feelings, but I'm afraid it gave my home town a bad image. And it may encourage vote-seeking politicians to oppose the papal visit.'

'But some quite reasonable people would disagree with the Pope about birth control or the position of women.'

'I think the Pope's mistaken about birth control. He's a magnificent character but I'm not sure he understands the ethical ambiguities of a free society. I don't think the papacy has grasped that there has been an explosion in human knowledge. It's much harder to believe these days than ever it was, but people must be able to make a choice. If love, not fear, is to rule the world, we must have freedom.'

Well, I thought, as I wrote down Dr Runcie's last sentence, that was as good an Easter message as anyone could wish for. It was a commandment on which we could all agree, whatever we might feel about God, and His responsibility for fear, or love, or both of them together.

Then the chaplain reappeared, and Terry Waite, the tall, bearded, lay diplomatic adviser who rescued the missionaries from Iran, and the teenaged children to whom the archbishop is clearly an amiable and greatly loved father. Dr Runcie's crowded day had started with prayers at seven o'clock in the morning. It was nearly fourteen working hours later, and time for his dinner.

He had the keys to Lambeth Palace, and led me out, past the wooden crosier in the umbrella stand, down the great staircase which led back into the world.

We talked about pigs, to which he is greatly attached, and he told me that he had been able to assure an anti-immigrant peer that P. G. Wodehouse's "Empress of Blandings" was in fact black. Dr Runcie is a man without an arrogant belief, humble before what he regards as a great mystery, tolerant in the way he believes God to be tolerant; an excellent priest who would no doubt make an admirable friend. Ex-Lieutenant Runcie had answered all my inquiries with honesty and great charm. But from his commanding officer, I thought as I looked up into the darkening sky over Vauxhall Bridge, from the real subject of my interview, I had had, to most of the questions I had so carefully prepared, a great deal of 'no comment'.

Tea with 'Dracula'

TONY BENN

'I thought,' I said to Tony Benn, 'that we might discuss Christianity. For instance, do you believe in God?'

'Christianity?' Benn started off with his usual enthusiasm. 'You know the bishops banned Tyndale's translation of the Bible. They didn't want the people to read Christ's social message.'

'Yes, but you were confirmed in Westminster Abbey. Do you . . .?'

'My father's beliefs came down from the Dissenters and the Levellers. My mother is a student of theology. At the age of eighty-four she's done a TV programme on the Prophet Amos.'

'Yes, but do you . . .?'

'I would say Christ's call to love your neighbour has more interest for me than the mystical side.'

'Do you believe . . .?'

'Ben Bella, the Algerian politician, was here the other day. In this room. After twenty-five years in prison. We were discussing the socialist basis of the revival of Islam.'

'But . . .'

'Reinhold Niebuhr, the theologian, was a great friend of my family, and he said: "It's the evil in man that makes democracy necessary and man's belief in justice that makes democracy possible." And *he* believed in original sin.'

'Put it like this,' I said. 'When you speak of bettering the people's lot, do you want to do it as a matter of human politics or because you're carrying out God's will?'

'Put it like that, I can't say it's God's will.'

Tony Benn

'So you don't believe in God?'
Tony Benn's smile is charming, extremely modest, even bashful.
'Put it like that,' he said. 'No.'

The Benn family's home in Holland Park shelters behind a small wilderness of a front garden, and the bench on which Tony proposed to his American wife Caroline stands surrounded by weeds and withering fir trees. The evergreen darkness extends into the house, where the passages are full of books, piles of old magazines and bicycles. In the front room the gloom is so prevalent that I almost felt called on to ask Mr Benn to light the row of miner's lamps, presentations to him from the lodges at various collieries. Among his art works are a nineteenth-century portrait of one of his wife's legal ancestors and a large drawing of Humphrey Bogart. I discerned, in the shadows, a collection of china mugs, someone's cello and plates decorated with pictures of Victorian politicians and the five imprisoned dockers whose cause Benn once championed.

'Tea or coffee?' Mr Benn had said as he opened the front door. He is a tall, handsome man with grey hair, a sun tan, a blue suit and large brown shoes. He looks well after his illness, although he still walks with a stick. Sir Keith Joseph called Tony Benn 'Dracula', but my first impression was of an articulate, charming and endlessly enthusiastic schoolmaster who went off hospitably, on my arrival, into some further darkness of the house to boil a kettle.

As my eyes grew accustomed to the gloom I managed to read the titles of the books: C. S. Lewis, Hazlitt, Tyndale's Bible, of course, and about six yards of *Hansard*. And then Mr Benn was back with a large mug, in which a tea bag swam until, with the aid of a spoon and a quick flick of the wrist, he sent it flying into the empty grate.

I had heard that Mr Benn treated writers for the newspapers with grave suspicion and turned on a tape recorder at the start of an interview. In fact he talked easily and trustingly, and not unnaturally our thoughts turned, in due course, to the leader of the Conservative Party.

'In some of the things you've said, I seem to detect a sort of sneaking admiration for her.'

'Not admiration, exactly. Mrs Thatcher is a formidable woman. I believe her policies are unjust and unviable, but she defends the class she represents with great vigour. This has the good effect of making our people feel that we should work as hard for the class *we* represent. She's really created three political parties: the monetarists, the corporatists and the democratic socialists.'

By 'corporatists' I understood Mr Benn to mean the Conservative 'wets', the Liberals and the Social Democrats. I raised the question of the SDP and his smile was undimmed.

'I think they'll become the biggest party in opposition to Labour. I mean the Establishment will never be so foolish as to allow Mrs Thatcher to destroy its interests. I believe it will start hedging its bets and back the SDP. It'll be one of those judicious withdrawals to a new position which the Right sees as inevitable.'

'The charge against you is that you've divided the opposition to the Conservatives. That by pressing the Labour Party to adopt your views you've made the world safe for Mrs Thatcher.'

'I don't believe we'll win the next election just by being against Mrs Thatcher. That's simply "Ya-boo!" politics. And we won't defeat her by repeating the old centralist ideas. We did that in 1979 and we went down to a resounding defeat. What we've got to do is meet her positive policies with a positive alternative. And if we don't do that,' Benn was drinking tea from his large mug, holding his pipe wedged under his knee and speaking with unfailing cheerfulness, 'we shall fall into that deep pit which is the middle ground of British politics.'

'Doesn't the present struggle in the Labour Party mean quarrels with old friends? Don't you find that painful?'

'Not at all.' He seemed surprised at the question.

'And what about the things Michael Foot, for instance, says about you?'

'I accept that as part of a normal political argument.'

'Are you happy?'

'Oh yes. Extremely happy.' Mr Benn was smiling and there was no reason whatever to doubt the truth of his answer. 'This is an important historical moment for Britain. A good time to be alive.'

'I hope this isn't an embarrassing question, but would you like to be prime minister?'

'Oh, I can answer that without any embarrassment. Yes.'

Born the second son of a Labour viscount, brought up in a Westminster house which was served by a daily cook, a cleaner and a Norland nurse, educated at Westminster and an ex-president of the Oxford Union, was not Mr Benn, I asked, inescapably middle class?

'Oh yes. I wouldn't dispute that at all.'

'When a majority of Bristol undergraduates voted for the Common Market, you said that they were clearly showing their middle-class origins. Do you think you can ever escape *your* middle-class origins?'

'I'm proud of my origins. But that's not what matters. What matters is whose interests you're going to serve. Who your clients are. My clients are the working people.'

'And you don't think being middle class gives you a rather romantic view of "working people"? For instance, you said that, when they'd thought about it, a majority of working-class votes would be against the death penalty. Do you really believe that?'

'When I was in Parliament at the time of hanging I felt a horrible sense of responsibility. For instance, I felt responsible when Ruth Ellis was executed. If working people had a bigger share in government and decision-making they'd feel that responsiblity and then I think their views would alter.'

'Aren't you ignoring the reactionary side of working-class opinion? There are quite a lot of Conservatives . . .'

'Everyone has a reactionary side.'

'You talk about the "working people" making decisions. In fact your system means that decisions are taken by the few Labour Party activists who bother to go to meetings.'

'There's nothing new about organizations being run by activists.

The law and medicine are run by a few activists who bother to turn up at meetings and sit on committees.'

'But what about the great majority of people who hate politics, who feel their time is much better spent mowing the lawn or making love or going to concerts or watching *Crossroads*? Who is going to represent *them*?'

'Look. We'll get our party in order and we'll turn up at the election, and then all the people who just want to cultivate their gardens have a perfect right to vote against us.' Mr Benn smiled with the modest satisfaction of a school captain who has just sent a rather mean ball gliding off to the boundary.

'But if you get into power' – I was staring, somewhat gloomily, at the portrait of Gladstone on a plate – 'won't I have to spend my whole life at ward meetings, participating in decision-making and all that sort of thing?'

'Oh no.' The school captain's voice was now gently reassuring. 'Not you. Of course you won't.'

'Once upon a time,' I said, 'you spoke of the duty of an MP to criticize his party and to be independent. Bernard Levin praised you for it. And now you want MPs to obey their local party committees quite slavishly.'

'Look. What we're doing is strengthening the power of Parliament and cutting down the power of a prime minister. British prime ministers have more absolute authority than medieval monarchs and they control a huge patronage. Do you know that prime ministers have made 640 peers in seven years, and it takes 40 million people to elect 640 legislators to Parliament? We want to end that sort of personal power and secret government which can spend £500 million on upgrading Polaris without even telling the House of Commons! Do you remember what Harold Wilson said about independent-minded MPs? He said they should remember they only had dog licences. Imagine the depth of contempt in that remark!'

'Burke said that an MP was a representative and not a delegate . . .'

'Burke!' Mr Benn's smile vanished. He looked, for a rare

moment, as though he were speaking of a man he genuinely disliked. 'Burke only visited his constituency once in six years.'

'All right. Assume you've got the form of decision-making you want. That's not going to cure our sick industries or produce jobs. What should all these decision-makers decide?'

'We're a very rich island, with coal and oil and all sorts of potential. I can't accept that old people still have to die here of hypothermia. I can't accept that we can't be prosperous. Investment has to be directed into our industries. There are millions of pounds lying on deposit, quite useless.'

'You mean you'd nationalize the banks?'

'At the moment banks are investing our money abroad, or buying gold, not exactly things which help industry or produce jobs.'

'And you'd introduce import controls?'

'In some way. After all, unemployment is already an import control. If you haven't any money you can't buy a Japanese television set.'

'And education?'

'With industry properly financed, with microchips and modern methods, we'd have labour and money to spare for the social services, for education, for the National Health and for twenty-four-hour care for the elderly. What do people do when they get richer? They spend their money on their children's education. That's exactly what the state should do!'

'When you were in government, did you find your plans constantly frustrated by the senior civil servants?'

'I had no trouble with my civil servants so long as they felt the prime minister was on my side. When they sensed that Wilson was against me, then they became difficult. It all comes back to the power of the prime minister.'

'You refused to join CND in 1959, and said it would split the Labour Party.'

'I saw it as a foreign-policy issue. But one changes over the years. Now I think I'd have marched to Aldermaston.'

'And the Common Market. You asked the people about that

when you insisted on a referendum, and the people were against you.'

'And I think the people made a mistake. The point about the Common Market is that it makes it illegal for us to govern ourselves, or govern ourselves well. Let me tell you about this. Heath introduced a small interest-relief grant for firms buying tools to raise North Sea oil. I continued it, and then I was told that I was doing something illegal and breaking the Treaty of Rome. The law officers got very nervous and said I mustn't do it. Do you know that the Foreign Office wanted me to have my Industry Bill approved by the European Commission before I presented it to Parliament?'

As always, when the talk turns to the Common Market, I felt overcome by torpor. I asked Mr Benn what he read, apart, of course, from *Hansard* and Labour Party pamphlets.

'Not enough, I'm afraid. Paul Foot sent me his book *Red Shelley* which I found fascinating.'

'And tell me this. Does it hurt you, being constantly presented to the public as a kind of mad Marxist werewolf?'

'Not really. Of course one is human, but I have so many friends. When I was ill I had 5,000 letters.' And Mr Benn was off to show his trophies; a beautiful brass model of a coal truck made for him by a disabled miner, and the embossed leather briefcase an ex-army sergeant made for him, decorated with pictures of the CND badge, and the bench on which Tony Benn proposed to his wife Caroline. He also produced a walking stick with a wooden miner's lamp handle, with which he posed as an improbable Beau Brummell.

'Tell me about the prime ministers you've admired.'

The answer was totally unexpected: 'Alec Douglas-Home fought a wonderful election campaign. He was out in the rain, plugging his message at street corners and outside factories, while Wilson sat in Transport House and gave WEA lectures.'

In the course of history less changes than we think. In 1931 Philip Snowden, an ex-Chancellor who left the Labour Party, said his former colleagues represented 'Bolshevism gone mad', and Herbert Morrison was said to carry *Das Kapital* into county council meetings and accused of joining the party only to infiltrate it with Marxism. Mr Benn is no doubt less of a wild-eyed European Trot. than a very English phenomenon: a descendant of the Puritans and the nonconformists and, despite his doubts about the Almighty, of the clean-living, nineteenth-century Christian Socialists. What the British people do with him remains to be seen. Will we pass him by? Or will we take the easy way to ruin a politician's reputation and eventually make him prime minister?

Mr Benn's great strength is clearly that he has brought a new excitement and moral fervour to politics. This may also be his weakness. The British tend to tire of their periodic bursts of moral fervour and long for the restoration of . . . perhaps some wetter, less formidable, jollier Queen Margaret the Second. Whatever happens, Benn is likely to be with us for a long time. Not for nothing is he the son of an eighty-four-year-old lady who has just made a television programme about the Prophet Amos.

The Sadeian Woman

ANGELA CARTER

'Did you get to like the Marquis de Sade?'

The slightly distraught, greying, pretty, high-voiced lady in the denim skirt, seated at her table in a cluttered Clapham kitchen, smiled at me with a certain tolerance.

'Really,' said Miss Carter, 'I don't see how anyone could fail to like the Marquis de Sade.'

Angela Carter's book, *The Sadeian Woman*, is the most perceptive study I have read on that singularly harmless and ineffectual aristocratic revolutionary (when he was made a judge for a short while during the Terror the Marquis de Sade was dismissed for being too merciful). 'I don't think de Sade enjoyed being a sadist,' Miss Carter smiled – she also has her moments of clemency. 'I think he thought it was pretty awful.'

Angela Carter and I sat together late one afternoon and I looked round at the 1930s wooden horse which had come from a roundabout, the piles of magazines, the coffee cups, and the framed print of the Martini horseman. We discussed a notable lady novelist and Miss Carter grew more testy than she had at any mention of the Divine Marquis. 'I can't do with *her*,' she said. 'Her books are all about preparing elaborate meals for men, or standing looking sadly out of the window as she scrapes the uneaten food into the tidy bin when they fail to turn up. I'd like to slap her little bottom for her.'

Angela Carter, at forty-one, must be the most stylish English prose writer of her generation. Her language is almost too perfect, and a prolonged submission to it is apt to leave the reader in a somewhat heady condition. Her books ('South American Magic Realism,' she murmurs almost disparagingly – 'nowadays everyone seems to be at it') are full of fairly innocent girls who suffer at the hands of Bluebeard or The Beast, or the alarming owner of an extraordinary toy shop. In her stories the woman is frequently the victim, fearful only that she may enjoy that condition too much. I wondered if this attitude didn't put Angela Carter somewhat apart from your every-day embattled housewife as seen in the women's pages of the *Guardian*.

'Feminists accuse me of being an "Uncle Tom", but I don't think I'd be the person I am if it weren't for the women's movement in the 1960s. I give readings to a lot of women's groups and the story of mine they like best is "Wolf-Alice". As a matter of fact it's about a woman being tamed.'

> She pawed and tumbled the dress the Duke had tucked away behind the mirror for a while. The dust was shaken out of it; she experimentally inserted her front legs in the sleeves. Although the dress was torn and crumpled it was so white and of such a sinuous texture that she thought, before she put it on, she must thoroughly wash off her coat of ashes in the water from the pump in the yard, which she knew how to manipulate with a cunning forepaw. In the mirror she saw how this white dress made her shine.

So Wolf-Alice grows to be a woman and the Duke, for his part, declines to a werewolf and is stoned by the villagers.

'About your father . . .' I sat drinking Miss Carter's tea and, helplessly male, had to borrow her pencil to write down her answers.

'He was a journalist on the news desk. He wore glamorous Edgar Wallace hats and smoked a pipe which he kept in the pocket of his jacket. He occasionally set himself on fire.'

'Were you in great awe of him, I mean, was he a Mr Rochester figure?'

'Put it like this, he was more like Mr Rochester than not. He was eccentric. He'd buy small-scale plastic chandeliers. He once bought a plastic parrot from Woolworth's, it was the sort of bird people put in their cages for real parrots to play with. He hung it up in the kitchen. I remember what my mother said.'

'Tell me.'

'She said, "Age cannot wither you, nor custom stale your infinite variety." '

'Quick with a Shakespearian quotation, your mother?'

'My grandmother was functionally illiterate. The whole family were heavily into the Independent Labour Party, which they managed to combine with the Church of England and lots of coronation souvenirs. They were classically hypocritical. My mother's a genuine radical. When I got into a direct-grant school in Balham she worried because she thought the educational standards might be brought down by the fee-paying kids I'd have to mix with. She stood firm and we were the last house in the street to surrender to a television set. Now the dreadful thing is, she's hooked on TV as though it were heroin.'

Perhaps it was her mother's heroic resistance to television that helped to make Angela Carter what she is, a genuinely and refreshingly literary writer, passionately dedicated to the construction of sentences. At the age of seven she worried about getting her first novel finished.

'It was a fairy story, of course?'

'Not really. It was full of social realism, cats going about their daily business.' Miss Carter laughed, and her laughter makes her seem much younger, a nubile girl perhaps, about to enter Bluebeard's castle in a spirit of gleeful apprehension.

'I read a lot by the time I was ten. Shakespeare and the Elizabethans. We had Shaw at home and I read it all. Now I can only remember the old men in *Back to Methuselah*. I grew into a very fat, lonely girl. Very isolated. But we had a wonderful French teacher. I read *Les Fleurs du Mal* and *Andromache* and they were both so exciting that I really got the feeling of being scalped.'

Later Miss Carter poured cider for me and I asked her if she thought sex, as I do, best regarded as a subject for comedy.

'The European tradition finds that very difficult.'

'You mean if you put a joke in *Les Fleurs du Mal* the whole damn thing might come crashing to the ground?'

'Yes, but then Charles Baudelaire wasn't famed for his sense of humour, was he? People didn't say, "Here comes Charles, let's have a rattling good time." '

I thought of Charles Baudelaire, with his *vrai toilette de guillotine*, as Angela Carter went off into peals of laughter. And I thought of her as a then anorexic young reporter on the *Croydon Advertiser*, listening to a record of Baudelaire's poems and 'singing along with it', as she told me, as other girls of her age might have done with Buddy Holly or the Everly Brothers.

'Is it very boring to be called a "woman writer"?'

'Unendurable! I think Christina Stead is just about as good as Conrad, but no one says that. Women are always compared to other women. Not as good as Virginia Woolf, or as good as Katherine Mansfield.'

'It seems to me that women writers aren't necessarily women. I mean . . .'

'I know! Dostoyevsky was the complete woman writer.'

'And Flaubert?'

'Flaubert was a drag queen.'

'And when you wrote about your misused heroines, were you writing about yourself?'

'Balzac said all fiction is symbolic autobiography.'

'So were you describing yourself as a young girl on the *Croydon Advertiser*?'

'Let's say I lived a rich fantasy life.'

'Dreaming of Heathcliff, the Demon Lover?'

'Or James Dean. The *poète maudit* . . . I had two characters I wrote about, the alienated youth and the bourgeois virgin.'

'And which were you?'

'Oh, both.'

'How did you discover your particular territory as a writer?'

'How can you ask that? It's like asking a cat what it feels like to be furry.' There was a pause and then she looked at me speculatively. 'I suppose you *could* go and ask a cat that.' Not me, I thought, the interviewer is helpless in the face of true writers, who are never able to explain their work in any words other than those of their books. 'All I can say,' Miss Carter stopped laughing, 'is that I try to understand about grammar from reading a lot of French. I try new constructions. Certain combinations of words act like a spell on me. Like a spell!'

'And do you still dream of meeting Heathcliff?'

'You know what they say about your sex life? You spend your first ten years trying to avoid getting pregnant and your next ten years trying to have a baby. Well, you spend your first ten years trying to meet Heathcliff and the rest of your life trying to avoid him. As a matter of fact, Heathcliffs are far too thick on the ground.'

When she let me out Miss Carter said, 'This is a typical South London hall, isn't it?' And so it was, with its accumulation of circulars and posters and bicycles and shopping bags and cardboard boxes. It was neither the entrance to Bluebeard's castle, nor the lair of a ducal werewolf. It was simply the home of a woman in her early forties who lives on her extraordinary imagination and her passion for constructing sentences: a true writer, something to be profoundly grateful for in this age of visual aids when the word 'literary' has become a term of abuse.

So I drove away through Clapham, leaving Miss Carter with her cats, her roundabout horse, the rhythms of Baudelaire and the shadow of the imprisoned marquis for whose ineffectual immolation of woman she can feel such pity and regard.

Unfulfillable Longings

ENOCH POWELL

'I can't forgive Harold Wilson,' said Mr Enoch Powell at a dinner a year or two ago, before a chat programme, 'for spoiling my opinion of the Emperor Diocletian.' It seemed that this emperor had withdrawn into private life at the height of his power, an action Mr Powell greatly admired until Harold Wilson followed suit. Now he was coming, slowly, to respect Mr Gladstone who never wanted to retire at all. When it came to the chat, I was surprised to find myself agreeing with Mr Powell on all the subjects except immigration, and even in that debate he startled the audience by what sounded very like a plea for miscegenation.

In a world of packaged opinions, when you only have to learn what a person thinks of fox-hunting to know his views on the death penalty, abortion, vegetarianism and women's lib, Mr Powell seems to me to have a marvellously unpredictable mind. I arranged to meet him again in a small, stuffy conference room in the Palace of Westminster. He sat beneath a portrait of Gladstone and thawed slowly.

'Fox-hunting? I approve of it as a social ritual; although if I thought that it involved cruelty to an animal or that those engaged in it derived pleasure from the prospect of cruelty, I should be against it.' The death penalty? 'So far as I can see, it has no effect on the murder rate. So it seems to me an avoidable brutality; and there are enough unavoidable brutalities in this life. I am a High Tory.'

'Does that mean you're a Christian?'

'I am an Anglican,' said Mr Powell carefully.

'All right then. Tell me about being a High Tory.'

'There's no such animal as an individual who exists without society,' Mr Powell insisted; and I thought of all those lesser Tories, and confused Conservative fellow travellers, who say that their creed is all about the individual and society counts for nothing. 'To me the second section of the Declaration of Independence is pure gibberish.' He pronounced the word with a hard g, making the liberal document sound particularly dotty. 'All that about being born equal and having a right to happiness! Rights have a meaning only within a particular society.

'Thomas More didn't opt out of Tudor society when he refused to affirm the king's supremacy in the Church; he died a loyal subject. You have to respect the law even to rebel against it. Criminals aren't anarchists!' Here Mr Powell allowed himself his first laugh, his pale face creased into a smile and his pale eyes sparkled. 'In fact, criminals are pillars of society.'

As this was a view with which I profoundly agree (I mean, where would barristers and judges be without criminals?) I made bold to ask Mr Powell a question. Did being a High Tory involve him in accepting a hierarchy? 'Of course, I always take my hat off to a peer. Even a life peer.'

'You mean you'd take your hat off to Hugh Scanlon, now he's a lord?'

There was a moment's pause; but the belief in hierarchy triumphed. 'If I happened to recognize him and I were wearing a hat at the time.'

Mr Powell's father became a pupil teacher in Birmingham in the 1880s. At sixteen Powell the older had to control classes of sixty children. He ended as an elementary-school headmaster. On his way up he met Enoch's mother, a supply teacher who taught herself Greek, went to church with a Greek Testament in her handbag and taught their only child enough to get him a scholarship to King Edward's School (in science, which his mother overdid as she knew it was his weakest subject) and a classical scholarship to Cambridge.

'I think my High Toryism is congenital, not hereditary. It's pure imagination to think we get our characters through the umbilical cord.'

In fact Mr Powell's father was a Lloyd George Liberal and his grandfather a Methodist lay preacher. His childhood seems to have been remarkably happy.

'Would your mother have been proud of your career?' I asked him.

'Her ambition was that I should be happy.' Mr Powell smiled at such a straight wish for a child.

'And are you?'

'Unhappiness, like grey hairs, is part of life. I am as happy as the human condition allows.'

I asked him about his declared belief in original sin. 'It accounts for juvenile delinquency. When I was young my friends weren't bored or idle or particularly poor; but we still took it out on the rolling stock of the Midland railway and vandalized it frequently.'

According to Mr Powell, society consists of a balance of all sorts of people. 'A nation consisting of nothing but VCs or arrant cowards would perish. In the same way there must always be dissidents, although no one can say how many are needed exactly.'

When he was young Mr Powell was apparently very musical and played the clarinet. Now he rarely listens to music. I asked him why not. There was a silence and the answer from this brilliant, isolated man was unexpectedly sad. 'I don't like things,' he said, 'which interfere with one's heart strings. It doesn't do to awaken longings that can't be fulfilled.'

The Prophet at the Ritz

MALCOLM MUGGERIDGE

'Could we meet in that tea place in the Ritz?' the blessed St Mugg. suggested. 'I find it's rather restful there.'

I expected to discover the contemplative seated alone beneath the large piece of gilded female statuary which dominates the Lapsang tea and cucumber sandwiches of his chosen cloister. Instead I found a couple waiting for me. The saint was elegant in a blue suit, up from his Sussex retreat in Robertsbridge and hot-foot from signing books at a literary luncheon, and Kitty Muggeridge, his gentle and still beautiful wife, was gazing thoughtfully at the Far Eastern businessmen and Sloane Rangers around us, giving the small guru beside her, to whom she has been married for over fifty talkative years, her occasional, amused attention.

'I suppose you want to talk about the porn we've argued about,' said Muggeridge, looking resigned. Indeed, we had once appeared opposite each other at a Cambridge Union debate on the obscenity laws. That was in the dear, dead days of the permissive society and part of an argument which is no longer of the slightest interest to anyone.

'Porn? Good heavens no. This is Easter. I want to talk about your spiritual progress.'

'That's a relief!' He looked at me, bright-eyed and patiently alert, with the sort of radiant happiness that comes only to those who have arrived hot-foot from a literary lunch and believe that Western civilization has collapsed, that their life's work has been trivial and unsatisfactory, and that most human activity is pointless and absurd, particularly, no doubt, when it consists of going to literary lunches.

'Your father was a Labour MP. Was he devout?'

'Not at all. But he saw Jesus as quite a good chap, perhaps as the honourable member for Galilee South, sitting in the Labour interest of course.'

'And your mother?'

'She came from Sheffield. She was more religious and more working class than my father. I once laughed at the story of Daniel in the lions' den and I'll always remember that she said, "If that's not true, then nothing's true."

'My father was a remarkable man. He left school when he was thirteen and went to work in the Radiac Shirt Company in the City as an office boy. In the end he was making £400 a year and they offered him a directorship. We lived in Croydon and his socialism was influenced by the nonconformist chapel rather than Karl Marx. He looked on the chapel as a valuable social centre where they had 'sham parliaments' and the literary society, and the minister was prepared to chair political meetings.'

Muggeridge *père*, it seems, was an entertaining speaker. He used to say, 'Isn't it extraordinary that we have *His Majesty's* Army, and *His Majesty's* Navy, and even *His Majesty's* Air Force, but we have the *National* Debt.'

On Saturday nights the twelve-year-old Malcolm would mount a stepladder in Croydon market and preach Universal Peace and the coming of the Socialist Dream in a piping voice against the roar of the traffic. Beside him a huckster used to sell shaving soap by covering his face with lather which he would then eat to prove its purity.

'Don't you regret all that early enthusiasm?' I looked back with affection at the young Muggeridge, convinced by Shaw and Wells, and his father, and the member for Galilee, that life on earth might yet be capable of improvement.

'Regret the vanished faith in Utopia? Not in the least. After all, Christ was offered all the kingdoms of the earth and he rejected them. Earthly kingdoms always have to be rejected because they're founded on power, and power corrupts. Of course, my father had a total faith in education. He despised the middle classes who lived on housing estates. I tried to point out to him that education would only turn the working class into a lot of complacent people who lived on housing estates. My poor father couldn't see that.'

'He didn't see that you can be wonderfully educated and still very unpleasant?'

'Well, exactly!'

'When did these religious feelings first come to you?' I tried not to make the question sound too clinical.

'I always had the sensation of being a sort of displaced person. I used to ask myself, "Who am I? What am I doing?" You remember what Lear says before he goes to prison –

> . . . Take upon's the mystery of things
> As if we were God's spies.'

Shakespeare's distracted monarch was, I discovered, deep in the mythology of the neat and carefully controlled Malcolm Muggeridge, the King of the Telly Interviews.

Muggeridge's father sent him to Cambridge, the Mecca of education, where he found himself the only state-educated boy in a wilderness of ex-public-school hearties. There he met Alec Vidler, a clergyman who had much influence on him, and Kitty, Beatrice Webb's niece, who no doubt had more. He went to teach at a Christian university in India and then worked for the *Manchester Guardian*. He gave up England to live in Russia, where he quickly returned to his normal state of amused disillusion.

'Why did you go to Russia?'

'I was convinced that the capitalist system had irretrievably broken down.'

'Do you still believe that?'

'Of course. More so than ever.'

'And do you still think that the Communist system has irretrievably broken down?'

'Oh yes. More so than ever.'

'So what's left?'

'It's the end of Christendom. From now on it's either the Gulag or the Permissive Society. I really don't know which is worse.'

The waiter had brought cucumber sandwiches and I bit moodily into one, trying to recapture the vanished optimism of past summers when Bernard Shaw came to tea with the Croydon Fabian Society.

'What about being a liberal?' I played my last card, knowing it was a loser.

'The fallacy of the liberal mind is to see good in everything. That has been of great assistance to the devil.'

'But haven't we made some progress? I mean we don't have public executions, and we've abolished slavery.'

'That sort of talk has to be watched rather carefully. I think you'll find there's more slave labour in Russia than ever before.'

'So there's no hope for us?'

'Oh no. None at all.'

Mr and Mrs Muggeridge were both beaming at me in high amusement. I thought that it had rarely been my privilege to take tea in the Ritz with such a deeply contented couple.

In his diary entry for 23 August 1936, Muggeridge writes of undertaking the mystic's 'long and arduous journey'. So I asked him, for clarification: 'Does that have anything to do with morality? I mean, can't you be wicked and still have mystical experiences?'

'It's like being an athlete. You have to have a régime. You must keep in training to get in touch with the infinite. Like a runner.'

'But could you behave badly and still be in touch with . . . whatever you said?'

'I did behave very badly, during the second time I was in India.' Muggeridge twinkled, no doubt recalling his romance with the difficult and tantalizing Amrita Shergil, described at length in his recently published diaries, a lady who had 'a certain genius but no taste, no values' and thought Ramsay MacDonald had 'a lovely face'.

'At that time,' Muggeridge said, 'I was carnally dead and spiritually blinded. I was experiencing hell, which is being imprisoned in the limitations of my ego.'

As he said this, Kitty Muggeridge looked at her husband and smiled at his memories of long past dissipation.

'Do you go to church?' I asked St Mugg.

'Not at all. I suppose I'm an Anglican but I always say if I'd been born on the banks of the Ganges I'd have been a Buddhist. Of course, we have the advantage of the revealed God.'

'Would you have liked to be a Catholic? Do you envy Graham Greene, for instance?'

'I'm very fond of Graham, but he relies too much on the magic of religion, which isn't a durable base. He's the sort of Catholic who regrets the end of fasting because it's no fun to eat meat on Fridays any more. I always said Graham is a saint trying to be a sinner, and I'm a sinner trying to be a saint. This annoys him very much, but really Graham has no talent for sinning.'

'And Evelyn Waugh?'

'Improbably enough I think Evelyn was genuinely religious. There was almost a saint inside him, or at least an awareness of what it's all about.'

What it was all about, I suggested to Muggeridge, was an omnipotent God who tolerates all the horrors that the sage of Robertsbridge finds so appalling, from the Gulag to the permissive society, and from television to mass murder. How could God permit, even by default, the extermination camps and the gas chambers?

'God seems to me to be an artist,' Mr Muggeridge said, 'rather than a judge. He has created the drama, and the parts of the play that are wicked and dreadful may be necessary to the whole creation in a way we can't understand. Life is a drama and not a progress.'

It was an idea that was new to me, that of the great dramatist of the sky working out his terrifying plots to entertain . . . well, to entertain whom exactly? Mankind, or a secret audience of mystics? Or perhaps Muggeridge's was a very old idea indeed, one more ancient and Greek than Christian. Whatever it was, it seemed a theory that fitted many of the known facts about playwrights and about God.

'We can understand the artistic act of creation, and it's the creation of a free will which comprehends suffering,' Mr Muggeridge said. 'Once the drama has been invented it has to play out its course. You know a nervous woman might have gone to Shakespeare and said: "Couldn't you have given King Lear some sort of pill or something so he didn't have to suffer so much, or provided an anaesthetic when Gloucester had his eyes removed?" And Shakespeare would have said, "Certainly I could have given King Lear a sedative, but then the play would have finished after Act One." '

'I can quite see why you don't like the idea of Utopia.'

'Can you?'

'Of course. Perfect societies would make very boring drama.' God the playwright, it was quite clear, had decided long ago that there was not much theatrical excitement to be got from the cautious approach of Fabian Socialism, nor any great tragedy to be derived from the life of Clement Attlee. 'Tell me. Do you really regret everything you've done in your life, as you seem to? I mean, hasn't life provided you with some useful drama?'

'Oh yes. Quite essential drama. It's no use asking people if they regret things. It would be like asking King Lear if he regretted dividing up his kingdom. I'm seventy-eight now and as a matter of fact I'm happier than I've ever been. The end of ambition comes as a great relief. And I'm happier than ever in the company of Kitty.' The Muggeridges smiled at each other, utterly contented.

'And after all that, is there a future life in your opinion?'

'Oh yes. No one knows quite what and we can't conceive it clearly. We may have glimpses of it, but it's beyond time, and we certainly don't know the full story.'

'Does the after-life have any sort of relationship to the way we've behaved on earth? I don't want to be crude about it.' I nervously approached a subject more embarrassing than porn. 'But do you believe in hell?'

'As I said, I've experienced hell already. I think our behaviour has a connection with our life after death, but no one can say what connection.'

'But life after death might be the perfect existence.'

'Oh yes. We can see perfection there.'

A perfection which might make, I thought, extremely tedious

drama. Could it be that the Eternal Playwright is, like the late Noël Coward, only really interested in life before death?

Tea-time was over, the Sloane Rangers and the Far Eastern businessmen were starting to order drinks under the demi-mondaine gilded lady, and the Muggeridges had to get back to Robertsbridge, to the English countryside which he loves and of which he is a part. I remembered the time when I was hard up and starting to write and Malcolm Muggeridge, who was then editing *Punch*, encouraged me by publishing some short pieces which I wrote about life in the law.

I remember the cartoon he liked but decided not to publish, which showed an elderly man sitting up in bed with his nubile bride and saying: 'Pass my teeth will you? I want to bite you.'

I remembered him laughing as though life on earth were a pleasure, even in the permissive society. I thought of how gleefully the twelve-year-old Malcolm must have announced Utopia from his stepladder in the Croydon market, and with what equal glee he has been denouncing it ever since.

And when I got home from the Ritz, there he was again; bright-eyed and articulate, talking at me from the television set in the corner of the living room surrounded by Kitty and Mother Teresa and his grandchildren and the poor of India, starving crowds who might, perhaps, not find material prosperity quite so vulgar and depressing as do their more spiritual mentors.

If God is an eternal Shakespearian dramatist, who, I wondered, is St Mugg? Is he old Pandarus, arranging an unlikely match between a materialist TV audience and the Mystic Experience? Is he Prospero who can cast his spell from the Magic Box and is often testy with the young? Or is he, perhaps, a never-ageing Puck, a less serious spirit and great entertainer, who plays endless tricks on our complacent vanity and retreats into the depths of the magic wood laughing at the world in general, but more particularly at himself?

Olivier Revisited

SIR LAURENCE OLIVIER

We were at the head of a valley and . . . grey and gold amid a screen of boskage shone the domes and columns of an old house.

So Charles Ryder, or Evelyn Waugh, came to Brideshead, and I came to Castle Howard, Vanbrugh's Yorkshire masterpiece where Granada Television – after a prolonged hiccough caused by the strike and a change of director – resumed filming Waugh's most popular and best-loved book, at a cost estimated to be nudging three million pounds.

This was my conversion to the baroque. Here under that high and insolent dome, under those coffered ceilings: here as I passed through those arches and broken pediments to the pillared shade . . . I felt a whole new system of nerves within me . . .

'The butty wagon's over there. Would you like a sausage and bacon sandwich?' The familiar voice of an ASM from Manchester interrupted my nostalgic reverie.

The arrival of a film unit had made Castle Howard look like Brideshead in wartime. The vans and catering wagons were drawn up at the front of the great, golden façade. The crew in bright anoraks, woolly bobble-hats, jeans and gum-boots looked like a regiment reduced to an informality Waugh would have censured. I was there on a visit, having written the screen adaptation of the luscious work in progress.

A writer on a film location, I reflected, as I bit into my sausage sarnie, is like an extra member at a wedding. He is always in the way, standing on a cable, vainly trying to hear a line of his dialogue that no one has bothered to change.

I got another cup of coffee from the butty wagon. The truth was that I had a slight hangover, having dined the night before with the father of the family of actors now inhabiting Castle Brideshead–Howard, Lord Marchmain–Olivier himself.

A long and triumphant battle with illness had sharpened his features. He had less hair than when we first met, some ten years before, and was wearing thick-lensed spectacles. But when Lord Olivier talked about acting, his voice still had its full range of inflections, he laughed, sounded young again, imitated everybody and acted all the time.

So at dinner in the Worsley Arms, over the sole and white Burgundy, we discussed the terrible scream that blinded Oedipus gave at the New Theatre just after the Second World War.

'It wasn't an "ah", or an "ugh" – more an "err",' he said.

'What was wonderful,' I remembered, 'was the endless pause, before you felt the pain.'

'Hardly new. It's exactly the same as timing a double-take in comedy. You know what I had to do to make that pain sound real? I had to think of animals. I thought of foxes screaming. With their paws caught in the teeth of a trap.' He held out his wrists, stiff and helpless. 'And then I heard about how they catch ermine. It was a great help to me when I heard about that.'

'How do they catch ermine?'

'You don't know?' Lord Olivier looked at me in amazement. 'In the Arctic they put down salt and the ermine comes to lick it.' He became a small, thirsty animal. 'And his tongue freezes to the ice. I thought about that when I screamed as Oedipus.'

Olivier's father was a vicar who preached with a high sense of drama. At a remarkable London choir school the future Oedipus had played Brutus at nine and starred as Katharina in *The Taming of the Shrew* at fifteen.

'When I was a child I lied all the time. "No. Mummy, of course I didn't. Why ever should you think a thing like that?" ' He acted the over-innocent performing schoolboy he once was. 'My dear mother whipped me for it. She didn't realize that I was simply training as an actor.

'I was always amazingly lucky. When I started there were reps in every town, two or three theatres. I began in a bad way, acting in all sorts of places. Do you know, I've actually played swimming baths, and the Town Hall, Staines?

'But I'd played Vanya and Parolles in Birmingham Rep by the time I was twenty-four, and Hamlet when I was twenty-eight. *Hamlet*'s the first real play, Shakespeare's only tragic hero who understood his own fatal flaw.'

He began to say the lines, quietly but as excitingly as ever:

'So oft it chances in particular men
That for some vicious mole of nature in them . . .
Shall in the general censure take corruption
From one particular fault.

'You have to use every sound in your voice for *Hamlet*. In *Richard III*, I only used three notes. I based it on imitations I'd heard people do of Irving.'

We had moved on to the Stilton, a bottle of claret and a story about a rival Shakespearian actor who had certainly seen all Olivier's great roles in the New Theatre season – Oedipus, The Critic, Richard, Vanya and the small part of the button moulder which he played in Ralph Richardson's *Peer Gynt*.

'I was writing letters in the Garrick when this furry hand fell on my arm and as I looked round into this pink blob of a face it said, "Hullo, dear boy, I loved your button moulder."

'Chaplin talked very pretentiously in his half-American, half-Cockney accent; but of course he couldn't escape from the unlikely fact that he was a genius. I remember him saying, "Hamlet was a young man who was subject to all youth's . . . *stimuli*." '

'Well, years later I used the same rather pompous inflection on the word *anthropophagi* in Othello's speech to the senators, so Charlie Chaplin got me a nice laugh.'

We had another bottle of Morgon and he talked about his

children, his son Dickie sitting his Oxford entrance. 'I hope to God he's a writer. Actors aren't really creative.'

'You don't think your remembering a frozen tongue during Oedipus' scream was creative?'

'Anyway,' the actor remembered his writing career, 'I worked with Terry Rattigan for weeks on the script of *The Sleeping Prince* and he collected all the royalties. Of course, I adored Terry, but the writer always wins in the end. When I was a boy I admired Gerald du Maurier. He seemed to mutter on stage but he had such perfect technique.

'When I started I was so busy doing a du Maurier that no one ever heard a word I said. The Shakespeare actors one saw were terrible hams like Frank Benson.'

'Will you ever do a play again?'

'Now I think I might. I think I may have the guts.' He rubbed the brown sweater over his stomach. 'In the theatre you need all the guts in the world. You have to say, "Hey! Look at me. I'm dancing!" '

The next day Lord Olivier's hair was whitened at dawn and by ten o'clock he was Lord Marchmain, the father of the Flytes who, at the end of a long quarrel with his wife and his Church, was dying on a huge, curtained four-poster in the Chinese Room at Brideshead. The resonant speech was as moving as ever, the actor's genius totally undiminished.

I had asked him what he was doing after *Brideshead*. 'God forgive me,' he said, 'Al Jolson's Jewish father.' At lunchtime he had a bowl of soup, a glass of new Beaujolais and a nap. Then he was driven, in his silk dressing gown, to be photographed on the steps of Castle Howard for the benefit of the readers of the *Sunday Times*. It was a brilliantly freezing November day and he made a joke.

'And did you know,' he said to no one in particular, 'that just a week after that photograph in the *Sunday Times* he died of pneumonia?'

Huddersfield Road, Camelot

ARTHUR SCARGILL

'Would you like to be a Labour MP?'

'I thought you quite liked me until you said that.'

I was asking King Arthur if he'd care for a post as a corporal. He has been offered four safe Labour seats, but why should he forsake the reality of union rule for the pallid pretensions of Westminster? It was a tactless suggestion and I felt like a guest at the Round Table who had committed some social gaffe, such as belching in the presence of Guinevere or spilling the gravy on Sir Lancelot du Lac.

'I can pick up the phone here and get things done,' I was reminded by His Majesty. 'An MP can't do that, can he?'

He spoke quietly, quickly and with boundless confidence. I knew I was in the presence of power. I had come to Camelot.

That royal residence, as everyone in the Yorkshire coalfields knows, is the National Union of Mineworkers building at 2 Huddersfield Road, Barnsley. It's a small enough castle, but with spires and crenellations, built around 1870 at the peak of the Tennysonian dream. Scarlet colliery banners hang in the great hall. Shields and heraldic devices are supported by statues of miners stripped to the waist.

'That man seems to have six fingers,' said Mr Scargill, who is sometimes known as 'King Coal' but more familiarly as 'King Arthur'. 'I don't know if the artist was drunk or if he just couldn't count.'

Despite the gothic dream, the building hums with efficiency, with its files of microfilm and its legal department dealing with a record number of compensation cases. We passed the secretaries who sit in Scargill's office. 'The girls are more left wing than I am,' Scargill jokes. 'All raging feminists – dead against my pin-ups on page three of the *Yorkshire Miner* . . .'

'So far as I can discover, I'm the youngest ever president of the mineworkers,' said Mr Scargill, who was then on the eve of his forty-fourth birthday. 'All the rest were grey beards around sixty-five. Yes, I'm an only child. My father worked all his life in the pits, except for a time when he was conscripted into the RAF. He wanted to be a rear-gunner but they found he was colour-blind. He had more influence on me than anyone. Not directly – he never told me anything directly – but he read about eight books a week. The house was full of books, the Bible, Shakespeare, we had everything. My father still reads the dictionary every day. He says your life depends on your power to master words. I read Jack London and *The Ragged Trousered Philanthropists*. Those were the books that formed my political opinions.

'I couldn't understand why they were burning wheat in the steam engines in Canada while half the world was starving. I decided to join the Labour Party, so I wrote to them. No reply. I wrote to the *Daily Herald*. No reply. So I wrote to the Communist Party. They sent round a wonderful man called David Larder who'd been dishonourably discharged from the army in Kenya because he refused to shoot coloured workers who were accused of belonging to the Mau Mau. He had a great influence on me. So I discussed it all with my friend Derek Stubbings and we signed up with the Communists.'

By a lucky chance Mr Scargill happened to have the old minute book of the Barnsley Young Communist Party to hand. He found me the entry for 31 March 1955, which read: 'Today the comrades visited Billy Smart's circus. Arthur Scargill and Derek Stubbings joined the party. The membership is now 11.'

'How old were you then?'

'I was fifteen.'

'And working?'

'When I left school I applied for a job in a factory. I thought I was the greatest gift to engineering since the invention of the wheel. Somehow no one seemed to agree. Are you nodding at that, Jean?' Mr Scargill said to the secretary who'd brought in our coffee. 'So I went into the colliery. Not the one in our village, but at Woolley, where I calculated the shift was half an hour shorter.

'I got up at four to walk a mile to the bus. We were in the engineer's office at six in the morning and he came in, a big man in a brown suit with oilstains on it, a brown pork-pie hat and thick glasses. His name was Lomas. "I want no bloody trouble from any of you." He glared round at us fifteen-year-old lads. "You do a six-hour shift and your snap time is twenty minutes. If I get any bloody trouble you're on your way. All right. Take them away." '

Mr Scargill's description of his first day at work is a set piece, Dickensian, well worked out, but all the same, worth listening to. If householders suffer power cuts through a miners' strike any cold winter, they may feel that Mr Lomas has a lot to answer for. And the same goes, undoubtedly, for Alf Melson.

'Melson used to stalk up and down a sort of raised gantry in the screening plant. He looked down at us with one eye. He was just like Captain Bligh glaring at his crew. We were picking bits of stone and rock out of the coal as it passed us on conveyor belts. The place was so full of dust you could barely see your hands, and so noisy you had to use sign language. When it came to snap time your lips were coated in black dust. You had to wash them before you could eat your snap.'

Later, at the pit bottom, where ice used to come crashing down the shaft in winter, and there were icicles a foot thick, the young Scargill looked after a pony.

'Appropriately enough,' he said modestly, 'its name was King.'

The office was quiet. There was a big, rather good oil painting of the young leader making a speech. In a corner an electric fire glowed beneath transparent lumps of plastic coal. Scargill, in a blue pin-striped suit, white shirt and crested tie, sat behind his desk looking like a successful young North Country solicitor or an up-and-coming officer in the serious crimes squad.

'Dad's a pretty hardline Communist still,' he said. 'He takes the Russian line on Poland.'

And his mother?

'She died when I was eighteen. She doted on me. She was a very religious woman. Of course, she had a brother crippled for life and a father who died at forty-four from working in the pit. But all she wanted was for me to have a safe job. She didn't want me in the Young Communist League. She thought it would lead to trouble.'

'Are you at all religious?'

'I certainly think Jesus Christ existed. And I remember this when they say I have unpopular views. When Christ was about to be crucified he couldn't even find a seconder, let alone anyone to vote for him.'

I turned, reluctantly, from further speculation as to how Scargill might have handled a Galilean block vote.

'You got involved in the union?'

'As soon as I started working. They were letting the faceworkers go earlier than us at the pit bottom so I put our case to the manager. He was a huge, pipe-smoking man named Fred Steele. When I'd finished talking he said, "I can't agree," and walked away. Then I realized he hadn't said, "No." "I can't agree" doesn't mean "No", does it? So I reported back to the lads and we left early and no one ever said anything about it.

'Then I complained about the ice down the pit. One of the managers said: "Oh, and I suppose a smart Alec like Arthur Scargill knows what to do about it." So I suggested they might have machines like big blow-dryers pumping hot air down the shaft, and that's what they did eventually.

'Of course, in those days, the union leaders were well to the right of Genghis Khan. I don't know if they were corrupt, but they were bosom pals with management. When I first got up to address a union meeting on conditions of training the chairman walked out after two minutes.'

'You left the Communist Party in 1961. That wasn't because of Hungary?'

'Oh no. I supported the Soviet Union over Hungary. The Hungarian revolution was joined by known Fascists. Quite different from the situation in Czechoslovakia. No. I disagreed with the Russians not allowing dissidents to leave the country. I'd give all dissidents free passes to get out as quickly as they could.'

No doubt Mr Scargill felt the same about Roy Mason, the local right-wing Labour MP, and all Social Democratic Party members. He was speaking as Henry V then, not King Arthur. 'Let him depart, his passport shall be made . . .'

'I also objected to the moving of Stalin's body outside the mausoleum and changing the name of Stalingrad. It would be like us trying to pretend Churchill never existed. It was distorting history. And I didn't like the personal discipline of the party. They wanted me to sell the *Daily Worker* on Fridays, but I had union business to look after on a Friday so I joined the Co-operative Party.'

Arthur Scargill was then twenty-three. He had become a member of the national executive of the Communist Party when he was sixteen; he was a young man with a long experience of politics. When he became a union official, he was able to have his father properly medically examined. Harold Scargill was found to be suffering from chest complaints, high blood pressure and arthritis.

'You said you believe in action outside Parliament. What's that mean exactly?' I asked King Arthur.

'Many of the most important political movements have been outside Parliament: the Campaign for Nuclear Disarmament, women's suffrage, Chartism and getting votes for working people. The Tolpuddle Martyrs, who started trade unionism, were not members of Parliament. MPs get constitutionalized out of existence. I'm not a great believer in an exclusive club in Westminster. Look, Mrs Thatcher only got 46 per cent of her electoral vote. I got 70 per cent of mine!'

'That's the sort of talk that gets left-wing candidates into trouble with Michael Foot. Are you disillusioned with Mr Foot as leader of the Labour Party?'

'Not disillusioned – just sad. I didn't support Michael to have him go with the right wing. You see, all power is with the people, in Poland and Bolivia and Chile . . .'

Not perhaps countries with parliamentary democracy, I was about to object, but Mr Scargill swept on.

'I predicted violence in the streets . . .'

'You welcomed it?'

'No, no – predicted it. I can't accept that judges have the right to override people's wishes in this country.'

'You assert a trade union's right to take political action?'

'Of course.'

'So a left-wing trade union leader should oppose a Conservative government?'

'Certainly.'

'But if you got your ideal Socialist state and you happened to have a right-wing miners' leader . . .?'

'A right-wing miners' leader?' Mr Scargill looked puzzled, as if I had imagined a Pope cited as a co-respondent.

'Would *that* leader be entitled to put pressure on a Socialist government?'

'It couldn't happen.'

'Why not?'

'Because rule three of the National Union of Mineworkers says that miners should join with other organizations to destroy the capitalist system.'

'But do you believe in free elections and political parties?'

'Of course. And I believe in proportional representation. In the end I think political parties may disappear. After all, they depend on classes, and if you abolish the class system, you should get rid of party politics. We don't need more than one union for the mineworkers, although we have political differences as big as mine and Joe Gormley's.'

'Do you agree with Solidarity's opposition to the Polish government?'

Mr Scargill looked doubtful. Solidarity, it seems, was not quite as bad as the SDP, but all the same . . .

'Solidarity's not a trade union. That's been clearly established.'

'You're saying it's a Catholic, reactionary movement,' I suggested; and Mr Scargill didn't dissent.

'You wouldn't outlaw other political parties in England?'

'Oh no, not outlaw them.'

The voice was reassuring and I was wondering how much political dissension there was at Camelot. Didn't Lancelot eventually put up as opposition leader?

'Doesn't it worry you that your and Tony Benn's politics are unpopular?'

'Of course they're unpopular. We want to change the system. If you want to keep things as they are, vote for Shirley Williams.'

'And your latest offer from the Coal Board?' I returned, finally, to Mr Scargill's job as a union leader.

'If our claims were met in full we'd be paid less than West German miners. If coal had the same subsidies as in all Common Market countries, we would be paid properly. As it is, the government's importing foreign oil at 30 per cent above cost. It's a crazy situation. It about meets the criteria laid down by Nero's sister and all the other senators who fiddle while Rome burns.'

When Mr Scargill rose to see me out he appeared smaller than I had thought, and his blow-dried hair was laid out in a neat pattern from the crown of his head. He still lives in a Barnsley bungalow with his wife, daughter and father. Now he is president of the mineworkers he will have to go south, not to Surrey, which he thinks is full of ad-men and the SDP, but to London. It's a move he regrets. The North, he says, is more realistic.

He loves traditional jazz. His car often rocks to the stereo recording of the *1812 Overture* played by three brass bands. He drinks an occasional half of lager and ducks out of official dinners.

Various people have found that he can be funny, charming, ruthlessly ambitious and 'as English as Yorkshire pudding'. His imitations of his predecessor Joe Gormley and of Clive Jenkins, the general secretary of the Association of Scientific, Technical and Managerial Staffs, are so good that he was asked to repeat them on television. Wisely he declined. It's not easy to combine the roles of Mike Yarwood and King Arthur.

As I left he showed me the photograph of one of his most notable battles – when he joined the flying pickets outside the Saltley coke depot at the time of the great struggle against the Heath government. In the general *mêlée* he had fallen to the pavement.

'That's the only time,' he said, 'when you'll see Arthur Scargill on his knees.'

On the way to catch a train I discussed politics with a mini-cab driver, a thoughtful man. 'This is a great country,' he said. 'I knew it was a great country when someone from the lunatic teapot party, or whatever it was, was allowed to stand in the Crosby by-election.'

We drove past Barnsley main colliery to Sheffield, where more and more factories are closing. The great problem of our time is, no doubt, to discover a way of combining a greater degree of social justice with political freedom. I suppose a smart Alec like Arthur Scargill reckons he knows the answer.

But what of the lunatic teapot party, I was left wondering, as I travelled south, towards Surrey and the ad-men, leaving King Arthur with another twenty years in politics and 70 per cent of his union vote.

The Secret Name

GRAHAM GREENE

The windscreen wipers whined like children in pain all the way up the motorway, and the rain soaked the piles of rusty earth as I drove into Leicester. The hotel was full of bright young men in three-piece suits attending a congress of shoe salesmen. Only the sign that it was the headquarters of the Leicester Magic Circle gave any hint of the Miraculous. Going up to the third floor I saw a notice which read, 'These lifts are not to be used as a means of escape.'

In the double bedroom one of the beds had been lain on. There was a silent TV set and a tray for making your own instant coffee. Graham Greene came out of the bathroom. He was very tall and stooped a little. His eyes were greyish, curiously transparent. He was wearing a brown sweater with a zip, fawn trousers and no tie.

'Do you mind having the whisky out of tooth glasses?' he said. 'I've washed mine.'

'I hate Greeneland. I had an outburst when *Horizon* wrote about it during the war. I didn't invent the world I write about. It's all true. The dead baby in the ditch in Indo-China is true! It's not part of the scenery of Greeneland.' Mr Greene spoke, not savagely, but bubbling with enjoyed indignation. He had come from Antibes to the English Midlands for the production of his latest plays, a double bill which marks his hilarious entry into the theatre of the absurd. London managements, to their discredit, having declined to do the plays because of their length, they had been snapped up by the astute Haymarket Theatre in Leicester for their small studio.

'The plays are on the manic side of my writing, like *Travels with My Aunt*. In fact I dreamed the curtain raiser.'

'I only dream on holidays,' I told him.

'Keep a pencil by your bed. Then you can write them down in the morning. The other night I dreamed I was going to meet my old governess, with whom I was passionately in love when I was a boy. Luckily I woke up. She'd be an old woman of eighty now. What could I have said to her?'

I poured more whisky into my tooth glass and nerved myself to mention a topic which I thought he might dislike discussing as much as he did Greeneland. Not, I assured him, that I wanted to argue about the existence of God. After all, as Mr Greene has said, neither of us would have to wait very long to find out.

'Antonia White told me that she asked an old and devout priest to remind her of the proofs of God's existence. He said that he knew there were some but had forgotten them long ago.'

'Do you think a belief in God is a great advantage to a writer?' I looked at him, and tried to keep the envy out of my voice.

'Oh, I think so. I've always felt it was having no belief that makes the characters in Virginia Woolf so paper-thin.'

'Someone said of Auden that he didn't love God, he just fancied him. Something like that,' I remembered.

'They might make the same charge against me. They say that I use religion to help my books. I think religion uses me. In *The Human Factor* there's a scene when Castle goes to see a horrible priest. He goes away uncomforted and then he sees someone else waiting to see the priest: "Another lonely man." I never meant to put that last bit in. My religion made me.

'I think this Pope's hopeless about contraception, but I can understand him wanting to keep the doctrine clear. Catholicism's about hard facts. You know the story in St John's Gospel, when he ran to the tomb at the time of the Resurrection? The beloved disciple was running behind him, but he caught him up and passed him and got there first, and found the sheets piled on the left-hand side of the cave and so on. It's because it describes one disciple catching the other up and passing him that I know it must be true.'

Either that or St John wrote fiction as finely as Graham Greene, I thought, as I topped up the tooth glasses, and asked him about England's most ornately Catholic writer.

'Evelyn Waugh was a strange man. I was very fond of him and I only saw him rude and arrogant once. It was at a dinner given by Carol Reed and his wife Pempe, and Alexander Korda brought his young mistress whom he afterwards married. Evelyn was horribly rude to this girl and, when I asked him why, he said, "It was dreadful of Korda to bring his mistress to Pempe's house." "But Evelyn, I brought my mistress," I told him. "That was quite all right. Your mistress is a married woman." Evelyn had a strange sense of Catholic morality. When I wrote *A Burnt-Out Case*, he said I was the lost leader because I'd exhausted my faith. But I hadn't lost faith, my character Querry lost his faith. Nothing to do with me.'

I remembered a similar mistake the over-ingenious Kenneth Tynan had made when he took the dog in Mr Greene's play *The Potting Shed* for God.

'Absolutely ridiculous!' Graham Greene was bubbling at the joke. 'It wasn't God at all: just a dog I had in Nottingham. It used to eat tinned salmon and be sick on the carpet. Shall we go down to dinner now?'

'Tell me about spies.'

We were waiting for the toast for the potted shrimps. 'We usually have toast with this,' Mr Greene had said, and it had caused consternation and a long delay. So we settled down to a bottle of dry Graves and a bottle of Côtes du Rhône. At the next table a young man with frizzy hair sat alone, listening to our conversation.

'Kim Philby wrote to me and said I had greatly exaggerated the bleakness of the Russia my leading character Castle found when he defected in *The Human Factor*. Philby said that when he arrived in Russia they presented him with two shoehorns. He'd never had two shoehorns in his life before. I think they're keeping Kim pretty busy now; the last postcard I had from him came from Havana.'

During the Second World War Mr Greene found himself, as a result of a mysterious process of selection, a secret agent in Freetown, West Africa. His job was to spy on the Vichy colonies.

'Did you achieve much?'

'Absolutely nothing! I had a perfectly good scheme to have a black Communist rescued from prison by pretended Communists. He'd be allowed to escape to French Guinea and give harmless information to the Russians. Then we'd say we'd denounce him to the French as a spy unless he gave us real information about them. The whole business was vetoed by Whitehall.'

'Perhaps they couldn't follow the plot?'

'I also planned to have a brothel opened in Portuguese Bissau. I thought that'd be a wonderful source of information; but Whitehall vetoed that also.'

'Do you think spies ever pass any important information?'

'I suppose Philby gave them the details of counter-espionage. Spies talking about other spies. Maclean had the atomic stuff . . .'

'Didn't you say you'd rather die in Russia than America?'

'That was misunderstood. I meant I thought I'd die quicker in Russia. At least they'd pay me the compliment of putting me in a labour camp. I suppose I'm on the left politically. I admired Hugh Gaitskell, but I couldn't stand Wilson and Callaghan. I'm very fond of old Communists, particularly at the moment when they're losing their faith.'

'You like anyone who's losing their faith?'

'I do rather. I knew an old Hungarian Communist, and I was very fond of him. I wrote to him about Clough's poem "Easter Day" where he says:

We are most hopeless who had once most hope
We are most wretched that had once believed

'I think he understood. He went round Hungary trying to buy the works of "Clogg".'

The young man at the next table got up and as he went out past Mr Greene he said: 'It was an honour to sit next to you.'

'Who was he?' Mr Greene speculated, greatly amused. 'Probably an American. Certainly a spy!'

'I don't really know anything about my characters until they get their names. In West Africa every boy has three names. One for his employer, one for his tribe, and his secret name that only his parents know. I have to find the secret name first.

'I just write in the mornings. Before I've washed or shaved or gone to the loo. Only about 300 words. I have to watch my characters crossing the room, lighting a cigarette. I have to see everything they do, even if I don't write it down. So my eyes get tired. You must find that, writing plays?

'I do the correcting at night, after I've had a drink or two. I find drink sharpens the ear. When I was young correcting always meant cutting down. Now it means adding bits in.

'What's writing? A way of escape, like travelling to a war, or to see the Mau Mau. Escaping what? Boredom. Death.'

When he was a boy in his father's school in Berkhamsted, Graham Greene read nothing but adventure stories, *King Solomon's Mines*, *Prester John*. As he grew up he announced he would be a businessman in China, defying his family who'd decided he'd be an author. The passion for strange countries and difficult beliefs seems to come from the boyhood terror of boredom, which led him to play Russian roulette with an old service revolver. At seventy-five Mr Greene still sounded like a boy, speaking of the risks he has enjoyed.

'I loved the Blitz. It was wonderful to wake up and know you were still alive and hear glass being swept up in the street. It was marvellous to walk down Oxford Street in the blackout and see the stars. I enjoyed the buzz bombs because you could hear them coming. I didn't like the V2s so much.

'When was I most afraid? I suppose in Indo-China when I was separated from a platoon of French paratroopers and found myself surrounded by Vietminh, or in the East End when the police charged at us after a Mosley march. But that's just panic. It doesn't last very long.'

In the summer Mr Greene leaves his small flat in Antibes and goes to Panama, where he's driven round by a part-time sergeant in charge of security who quotes Rilke. Or he's in Spain with a great friend, a priest who is also Professor of English at Madrid University. 'We fill the car with Castilian wine and my friend talks endlessly. I suppose, as you grow old, life becomes easier. Less unhappiness, less despair, less fervour and manic moods. Only the problems of living become more difficult.'

Some of the problems seem to have resolved themselves. He has had a steady relationship with a woman friend lasting over the last twenty years. 'I suppose such things are easier if you are heterosexual.' Mr Greene freshened the tooth glass and speculated: 'When I was at Oxford homosexuality was in fashion; but I was aggressively heterosexual, which was all right as long as you didn't do it. Peter Quennell did it with a girl who led a Borzoi about, and he got sent down. I only fell in love with girls at dances. And I am no dancer.'

Even though not a dancer, Mr Greene seems to have found some peace in France where he now feels more at home than in England. In the evenings he can be seen eating in a quiet corner of the restaurant Félix au Port in Antibes, reading from his small, twelve-volume edition of Chekhov's short stories. 'The only things that I really miss,' he said, 'are English beer and sausages.'

The Mission for the Deaf is a clean, new building on the outskirts of Leicester. Inside there was a smell of furniture polish, a lot of echoing noise, a modern chapel and a hall where the actors were rehearsing *Yes and No*, Mr Greene's curtain raiser. The play is very funny, a joke about pretentious directors and theatrical knights. Mr Greene sat at a table, wearing horn-rimmed spectacles, finding improvements for his script. When the run-through was over, Robin Midgley, the director, said how grateful they all were to their author for coming to Leicester and spending ten days at rehearsals.

'Of course I came,' said Graham Greene. 'How else am I going to learn my trade?'

'Good-bye,' I said. 'I'm not feeling quite myself this morning.

But I enjoyed our dinner enormously. Let me just make sure – your new book's called *Dr Fischer of Geneva or the Bomb Party*?'

'That's it. The idea came to me at Christmas dinner with my daughter. When we had crackers. Then I've got a book of essays coming next.'

'*Ways of Escape*?'

'Exactly. And now I've got an epigraph for it. Remember the notice in the hotel? "These lifts are not to be used as a means of escape." '

When I drove back down the motorway the sun was shining. I thought of Mr Greene sitting at his table in the Mission for the Deaf and how he had achieved what I hadn't expected to find, a kind of happiness.

An Ironside Reborn

JAMES ANDERTON

'I'm a fatalist,' said Mr James Anderton, Chief Constable of Greater Manchester.

'I am too, sir,' said the young superintendent. 'I believe villains are fated to be caught. I honestly believe that.'

'Then why punish them,' I asked, offering my glass to be refilled with red wine by the attentive constable in shirt-sleeve order, 'if they're only doing what God ordained?'

'They have a choice when they commit crimes. All the same, I believe in destiny. And reincarnation.' The chief constable repeated that he definitely believed in reincarnation.

'So who were you in a previous existence?' I asked. Mr Anderton paused with a spoonful of grapefruit segments half-way to his mouth. He has well-chiselled features, very smooth hair brushed back and a somewhat marmoreal complexion so that he looks, if not exactly like a Roman emperor, then like the governor of some distant but well-organized province in further Gaul. He talks fast and copiously and smiles almost all the time. I wondered whom he was going to choose for an ancestor.

'Well,' he said, 'weren't we discussing Oliver Cromwell?'

That morning I had sat with James Anderton in his suite of offices on the eleventh floor of the modern glass-and-concrete police building, looking out over his domain, his patch, his manor. There was a fine view of Old Trafford and Manchester United Football Ground, the mucky no-man's-land between the canal and the second-hand car auction and, stretching away to the Pennines, the vast city, the Exchange Theatre, Granada Television, Moss Side and the streets by the Harp Lager factory where young DB2 Constable Anderton once plodded faithfully, dreaming of his past as an Ironside and his future perhaps in Manchester, or Scotland Yard, or sitting on the law-abiding side of the Great Stipendiary Magistrate of the Skies.

Manchester, as Jim Anderton points out, is in many ways England's answer to Los Angeles. It has almost as many inhabitants as the American city, only thirty more square miles and a police force of a similar size. And yet, in the serious business of crime, the English are amateurs. Los Angeles has 576 murders a year and Manchester can only manage 16, Los Angeles has 2,339 rapes and Manchester 37, and the American city has three times as many robberies and serious assaults.

Such is the comparatively trivial extent of crime in our country, yet these are the figures on which the Police Federation and those politicians who, bankrupt of more creative ideas, invoke the sacred name of the Great Goddess 'Laura Norder', trying to make our flesh creep and calling for stiffer sentences and the Return of the Rope. However, the need to make such demands lies far deeper than mere statistics, and after a morning spent in the Manchester Police Headquarters and lunch in the Senior Officers' Canteen, you feel that punishment is not so much a way of dealing with crime as a manifestation of the Will of God.

'But I am now totally opposed to the death penalty,' said the Chief Constable of Manchester. The charm of his company, which is undoubted, lies in the constant element of surprise. He had already waved from his window towards what he agreed was the hopeless filth and squalor of Strangeways Prison and had said that half the people in prison should never be there at all, although the other half should never be let out. 'I do believe hanging is unchristian and inhumane,' he went on. 'I do believe that God has prescribed hell for the wicked. I'm not sure that hell is after death. I think hell is the guilt that criminals suffer in this world. If they're killed, how can they suffer guilt?

'Out there,' he looked down on the hazy city, darkened with the threat of a storm, 'are young blacks whose families have lived here for generations. My family didn't live in Manchester, theirs did. They have more right to be here than I have. And what are we offering them? No jobs. No future. Nothing.'

'Then can you blame them for turning to petty crime?'

'We get as many crimes from the children of rich parents. School teachers', architects' kids, even the children of barristers.'

His pale eyes were fixed on me. I looked away at the group of photographs of his staff, of deputy and assistant chief constables in uniform, at the cups won by his force for rugby football and all-in wrestling. What mad passion of love was it, I wondered, that made me pinch the necklace from the Henley Woolworth's when I was eight?

'As for young people convicted of violence, I would be in favour of punishment with a medically approved cane.'

Almost half a century after my crime, I looked at him with apprehension. 'Really? Who'd you get to do it?'

'Anyone. Fathers beat their children, don't they?'

'In my case, absolutely not.'

'Then I'd do it. My father beat me.' The chief constable sat back, still smiling. He was in a civilian suit, without a jacket, with a little plastic card bearing his photograph and proving his identity clipped on to his tie. He had the look of deep and complacent satisfaction which men assume when they speak of having been beaten in childhood.

Mr Anderton's grandfather was unemployed, a fervent disciple of Keir Hardie. His father was a Wigan miner, and his parents were both religious, one Methodist and one Church of England, and staunchly Labour. He came from a small cottage, two-up and two-down with a communal lavatory, under the shadow of a tip.

'Did you play cops and robbers?'

'I don't remember. I was always a little leader. I was mischievous. We got boxed on the ear by the local police,' he smiled again. I thought it a curious thing, this great British nostalgia for ear-boxing bobbies.

'Did you ever steal anything?'

'Good heavens, no!' I believed he was telling the truth.

'When did you decide to be a copper?'

'After I got a scholarship to Wigan Grammar. I had this great love of humanity and a desire to stand up for the underdog. After school I went into the Military Police by choice.' He clearly had no doubt; no fear that what he had said might sound contradictory, or even comic. 'I thoroughly enjoyed my time in the army. Then I came out and joined as a copper on the beat in Manchester.'

No doubt it was the sense of mission as well as the ever-charming smile that gained the articulate Constable Anderton rapid promotion. By the age of thirty-five he was chief inspector in the Manchester City Police; by thirty-six he was assistant chief constable of the Leicester and Rutland Constabulary. He was assistant to the Chief Inspector of Constabulary at the Home Office and later became deputy chief constable of Greater Manchester.

He had got the job as ruler of the 10,000-strong Manchester Force, policing 2,750,000 people over 500 square miles, nearly four years before, when he was forty-four. 'My work is a joy,' he says, 'from first to last.' Each morning he bounds up to his office, greeting everyone he meets by name. He works an eighty-hour week and will never refuse a chance to talk in public to senior citizens or lads' brigades, or as a lay preacher on Sundays, or to appear on the telly or address international fire security conferences or crime prevention committees or Mrs Whitehouse's Viewers' Association on 'The Police as a Moral Force'. He climbs into uniform and visits his bobbies on the beat. Wherever he goes he spreads the doctrine of a God who walked the streets without any particular humility, saying to mankind the theological equivalent of, 'Now then, what's all this going on here?'

He raises, of course, considerable opposition, which pains him. One Church of England critic said that if the chief constable would stop preaching sermons he would refrain from becoming a part-time bobby. Mr Anderton found this remark 'incredibly rude' and said, 'When I hear things like this, I wonder what the world's coming to.' He may also enjoy the feeling of martyrdom that such gentle barbs can bring. 'Am I to be gagged because I happen to be a chief constable?' he says. 'I have withstood a veritable barrage of hostility and abuse, but I am a stronger person now. I can see a light shining ahead of me!' Church of England clerics are unhappily like barristers' children, part of the increasingly faithless middle class.

'Do you miss the actual detection?'

'Oh, yes. It's the hunt, you see. All policemen are hunters. And I'm still a sworn-in constable.'

'The hunt. Yes, sir. That's what it is,' the young superintendent agreed, looking back to his more recent past, before he became press officer, or police PR man, to Jim Anderton. Once the superintendent had to solve the mystery of a pub landlady, strangled, battered to death with bottles and stamped on. 'You command a force of about 200 men who are all knocking on doors, or collating information, or searching the scene of the crime. And what you've got to do is to stop them going off the boil when someone thinks they've found something. You get about three hours' sleep a night and by the time you go in to interview the suspect you've got the evidence you need.'

'How do you feel when you've got the man you've hunted? Do you feel pity?'

'No. And not anger. Not disgust,' the superintendent said. 'The hunt's over and you just feel cold about it.'

'What about police officers making up admissions? Verballing goes on, doesn't it?'

'I don't accept that,' said the chief constable. 'Anyway, it's much more effective to say a man just didn't answer, if that's the truth. It does him a lot more harm.'

'You don't believe in the right to silence?'

'No, I don't. I think the caution's a farce. This is what I believe.' We were back to the Creed of a Devout Copper. 'Everyone is accountable to God and his fellow men. So a man's silence should be some evidence against him.'

'How does that fit in with the law's presumption of innocence?'

'We owe God an explanation,' the Chief Constable repeated. 'He calls on us to explain our conduct, once it's questioned.'

I turned from God the Almighty Interviewer and asked, 'Don't you think police questioning should be conducted with tape recorders or video machines? We spend days in court and thousands of pounds challenging police evidence. If it was recorded, there could be no such questions.'

'No machine should be allowed to get in between the suspect and his interrogator,' said the chief constable with certainty. 'It would break that essential rapport which a detective needs to elicit an admission of guilt legitimately.' Jim Anderton spoke of that terrible moment when the questioners and the suspect are alone together with a kind of reverence; and as if I had suggested tape recorders to intrude on private prayer.

'But what would you do if you knew an officer was making up verbals, even when he thought the suspect was guilty?'

'He'd be out of my force.'

There's no reason to doubt Mr Anderton's hard line on police corruption. In the strict religious order of priests which he wishes to make of the Greater Manchester Force, frocks fall like autumn leaves.

'I've got rid of more officers than anyone in any other force. If an officer's accused of misconduct I conduct a trial from nine in the morning till 6 p.m. None of your 10.30 to 4 p.m. courtroom times. If they've been drunk, or told lies, or been guilty of violence, they're out. They get the chance to put their case, but if I think they're guilty, that's it.'

A Manchester landlord was recently prosecuted for serving drinks after hours at a birthday party. His customers unhappily turned out to be about twenty celebrating coppers who were immediately asked by Mr Anderton to resign from the force.

More alarming than this ruthless attitude towards policemen who prolong drinking-up time is Anderton's curious attitude towards those who criticize the police too vociferously. He is said to have predicted 'detention for political subversives' in the not-too-distant future if anarchy threatens, and 'political subversives' start to sound dangerously like those who won't stop rubbishing the Old Bill.

'Legitimate complaints are healthy and I think they might be investigated by the Ombudsman. But the mischievous knocking of the police is part of a concentrated campaign to undermine us.'

'Who do you think's organizing the campaign?'

'Extreme left-wing groups and factions in the ethnic minorities. People who are permanently hostile to the police and argue that the military forces are unnecessary. It's all designed to drive a wedge between the police and the community and provide a suitable climate for political activists. The aim is to overthrow the pillars of democracy.'

'The problem with Anderton,' says Jeff Willner, a defence lawyer who represents Moss Side for Labour on the Manchester District Council, 'is that he regards all criticism of the police as a sort of heresy. So his eyes are closed to what's really going on. In fact my young black clients have more complaints about police violence and victimization than ever. Anderton is complacent about the real feeling of minorities.'

I asked him what Anderton had achieved.

'Well, he's protected all the porn shops and a lot of clubs. He's very keen on enforcing the licensing laws. He does some rather strange things. One day he had policemen waiting at the traffic lights. Another time he filled a rather quiet district called Collyhurst with a lot of armed police. I suppose it was some sort of exercise, but we never found out exactly what. The manager of a gay club called Napoleon's was warned about "licentious dancing", but I can't say Anderton's particularly anti-homosexual.'

'What else has he achieved?'

'Well, of course, he's preached a lot of sermons and the Junior Chamber of Commerce have voted him "Manchester Man of the Year". I really think the police should stick to their job, which is simply the detection and prevention of crime. They shouldn't try to be social workers; still less does the chief constable figure have to be the fountain of good and evil.'

The chief constable, of course, won't have the charge of complacency. 'I just wish we had more West Indian and Asian recruits in the police,' he says. 'The West Indian boys won't join because of the disapproval of their peers. But those we've got are first class. We've got one Asian sergeant called Shaffique. An absolutely super chap.'

Jim Anderton, who has closed the porn shops and now sees Manchester as a far more 'decent' city than London, is angry with the report of the Home Office committee on pornography, chaired by Bernard Williams.

'As Freud taught us, in order to create a civilized society for culture to rest upon, people must respect each other and there must be a degree of discipline. The Williams Report is simply a waste of time and money. Even though it may have to be sold in plain wrappers and from regulated shops, porn will spread through this city.'

As he spoke and gestured to the hazy townscape below us, the chief constable seemed to conjure up a vision of a hundred school playgrounds, where the children sat thumbing eagerly through the Danish porn which leaked from the discreet shops planned by Professor Williams and his advisers. On this subject, Mr Anderton's language thunders from the pulpit. Porn merchants, he has told the Viewers' Association, 'are garbage in the sea of life and will not be content until nearly everyone else is floating like trash in the same filthy waters and lending credibility by majority numbers to their nefarious deeds'.

Although Mr Anderton dismisses the finding that crime and pornography are unconnected as unproven, which is probably true, he offers no real evidence for the view that erotic literature leads to crime. However, he says he has 'enormous, unsolicited public support' for his point of view; and his following in the Mrs Whitehouse constituency is obviously extremely strong.

A sense of dedication and ambition naturally go together. Mr Anderton has admitted his hope of becoming the next Metropolitan Commissioner. This prize has eluded him, but he has had his successes (he handled the National Front marches in Manchester in 1978 with a tact which avoided the kind of disasters which occurred in Lewisham), as well as his undoubted boobs, as when his men confiscated a book of *Page Three of the Sun Girls* from a local supermarket. Whatever happens, he will never be quiet. The photocopied speeches, interviews and lectures continue to stream from his press office. How does he take his pleasure?

'My wife is my love. My daughter is my future. My work is my best friend. I also enjoy walking in the wind.

'I do a lot of do-it-yourself. I've never employed a decorator in my life. And I'm a bibliophile. I've got books all over the house. I've got four or five books on the go in every room and pencils and notebooks to go with them. What do I read? Philosophers, Sartre and Kierkegaard.' Indeed, he may have once startled Mrs Whitehouse's followers by quoting Kant to them. 'Morality is not perfectly the doctrine of how we make ourselves happy, but how we make ourselves worthy of happiness.'

The chief constable, it seems, is also reading *Whatever Happened to the Human Race?* by Francis Schaeffer and Dr Everett Koop (a recent, personally inscribed gift from Dr Koop with whom he corresponded over their 'natural opposition to pornography and belief in humanity expressed through the life of Christ'), *The First Circle* by Alexander Solzhenitsyn, *The Climate of Treason*, *The Queen's Peace*, *The Fifteen Decisive Battles of the World*, and *Cromwell, Our Chief of Men* by Antonia Fraser, a birthday gift from his wife.

'What about music?'

'I love singing. I was a chorister when I was a boy. What about that Luciano Pavarotti? He came from a working-class home like I did, and what a voice! When I saw him on television, singing in church with his father, the tears came into my eyes. I couldn't see for tears. A little while ago I managed to get into the Manchester Exchange Theatre. We saw *The Lady from the Sea*. What a marvellous performance! What an absolutely super evening! No, you've got to admit it. There's absolutely no one in the world to touch Vanessa Redgrave!'

'Jim Anderton's a marvellous bobby,' said the sergeant who drove me back to Manchester Piccadilly. 'He's always got a word for you when he meets you in the lift. We're all worked off our feet, of course. I have to coordinate the work of the various divisions when it comes to royal visits, or processions, or demonstrations, or when the Bomb falls. Oh yes, at least I'll be safe in the shelter when the Bomb falls.'

Going back to London, I thought that meeting the chief constable was a valuable experience for a 'liberal' middle-class writer. Flamboyant puritanism and an exaggerated respect for authority is not something imposed from above, it's deep in working-class culture. Letters of support flood in on Jim Anderton, and he's not only the favourite of the Junior Chamber of Commerce but, as he proudly announces, he has his enthusiastic admirers on the North Sea oil rigs.

And the Chief Constable of Greater Manchester forces us to consider what sort of a police we really require. No one can argue that we can do without the police, but do we really need them as a 'moral force'? Should their leaders invariably be presidents of the Christian Police Association? Can it be said, as Jim Anderton told the National Viewers' Association, that the fuzz is 'the one profession best placed to set an example of integrity of purpose, honest leadership and natural justice untouched and uncompromised by any political pressure or factors'? Is that statement merely a comfortable bit of self-satisfaction, or could it be looked on as a bid for police power if political authority collapses? And anyway, do the Boys on the Beat really represent the Will of the Almighty? I found myself tempted to remind the chief constable that the Christian God chose to visit us in the form of a law-breaker and convicted criminal; he converted the centurion but hung beside the thief.

Perhaps the great decisions of our lives as to our religion or morality or personal conduct are taken far from the limited world of police control, and the threatening finger on the collar. Do not the law and the police work best as a humble public utility, like sewerage farms or rubbish carts, and become ineffective and possibly ridiculous when they try to enforce private morality or personify religious beliefs? The Chief Constable of Manchester would certainly disagree. He has little doubt on this, or indeed any matter. But he has, perhaps, forgotten the sentence which he used so effectively in a previous incarnation: 'I beseech you, in the bowels of Christ, think it possible that you may be mistaken.'

Birthday Greetings from a Monk

CARDINAL HUME

'How do you feel about dying?' I asked the cardinal. 'I mean, we must be about the same age. Do you think about dying a lot?'

'In fact we're not the same age.' The Cardinal Archbishop of Westminster, holder of the office established by Restitatus in the year 314, wearer, like Wolsey and Manning and the ancient poet Newman, of the hat from Rome, silver-haired, tall and extremely fit, sporting an old black pullover and a dog-collar, poured me another cup of tea and looked at me with a certain tolerance. 'You were born on 21 April 1923, I was born on 2 March. I'm about seven weeks older than you.'

What was this? An unexpected courtesy to that unwelcome intruder, the interviewer? A demonstration of the Church of Rome's attention to detail and excellent state of readiness for all comers? Whatever it was, it gave game point to the cardinal and made me forget my question. He reminded me of it gently.

'Ronnie Knox said everyone's afraid of dying but no one is afraid of being dead.'

I drank my tea, wondering what kind of comfort I could find in Monsignor Knox's little epigram.

'You know, you were born on St Anselm's Day!' The cardinal seemed to be finding my birthday a continued source of entertainment. 'Faith is seeking understanding. That's what St Alnselm said. And his day is 21 April. *Your* birthday!'

My quest for the cardinal had begun in Westminster Cathedral,

London's gigantic pile of Victorian Byzantine architecture, whose streaky-bacon towers dwarf the glass and concrete of the reconstituted Army and Navy Stores. In the marmoreal interior you can read the list of Catholic archbishops and cardinals, ending with Thomas Cranmer 1533 (deprived for heresy). 'The only good thing I ever heard about Cranmer,' said Hurrell Froude, pupil of Keble, friend of Newman and inspirer of the Oxford Movement, 'was that he burnt well.' After Cranmer, the Church went underground with a series of vicars apostolic under the immediate jurisdiction of the Holy See, until the Catholic liberation and the appointment, in 1850, of the voluminous Cardinal Wiseman whose Friday fasts were said to have a certain 'lobster salad' quality.

The list stretches on through Manning to Heenan and back to the disintegration of the Roman Empire; but the true Church has its own instinct for keeping up to date. Recorded pop music echoed round the cathedral on the day I visited it; a priest was discussing the arrangement of spotlights with an electrician in overalls. In a side-chapel there was an exhibition of photographs from El Salvador; bare-breasted ladies, some feeding babies, some just giggling and looking pretty, smiled from the walls. Archbishop Romero and a Pope from behind the Iron Curtain may have been two of Catholicism's greatest successes in the modern world. Another, strangely enough, may have been the choice of a Benedictine monk, ex-abbot and schoolmaster, who can look, in his television appearances, like a gentle ecclesiastic carved in Chartres Cathedral, to break the 'Irish tradition' and succeed Cardinal Heenan as the voice of Rome in Britain.

'I thought the boss might be in here,' said the little, grey-haired priest. 'If you come down now you can get a cup of tea early.'

I had walked away from Westminster Cathedral, down the back streets of Victoria, past the Cardinal pub and into Archbishop's House, which is huge, very dark and about as immediately welcoming as a North Country station hotel during a period of national mourning. I was waiting in a large empty room which might have been the residents' lounge, a room which no wife ever tidied, where a small electric heater stood in a cavernous fireplace and the glass ashtrays were kept clean by nuns.

'People exaggerate when they talk about the tomb-like loos in this house,' said the small priest, who had won himself a plastic mug of tea. 'Although there is one upstairs which makes you think you're sitting on a pedestal.'

The cardinal now came in and led me to a smaller, cosier room, with brighter pictures, where tea in china cups was brought in by a nun and the cardinal stood to take the tray.

'Could we start at the beginning? Your father wasn't a Catholic?'

'No. Only my mother. My mother was French.'

George Hume's father was Sir William Hume, a distinguished physician, and the cardinal's Durham background is comfortably middle class, as was his education at Ampleforth, where he was captain of the First Fifteen, a fast bowler and the organizer of concert parties to tour the local villages for charity. In 1941, at the age of eighteen, he became a novice monk and took the name of Basil.

'It was a terrible choice. The war was on then and I didn't know whether to go into the army or become a monk. If it happened again I think I'd have gone into the army.'

From Ampleforth boy to Ampleforth monk, from schoolmaster to abbot to archbishop: Cardinal Hume is ready to admit that it has been a sheltered life, just as he agrees that his celibacy may have its drawbacks when he has to pronounce on sexual matters.

'It was a difficult time. I should have liked to have gone as a soldier.'

'You're not a pacifist?'

'Not in the least.'

'Did your father disapprove, when you became a monk?'

'Oh no. But when he drove me to the station he made me promise to come out if I couldn't stand it.'

'Were you ever tempted to come out?'

'Oh, all the time. But I told an old prior who was ill about my temptations, and he said, "Don't decide to leave until I come back from hospital." Well, he never came back from hospital and so I never left.'

The Benedictine Order is moderate and has never been particularly rigorous. At Ampleforth the monks can be seen sitting at ease, saying in soft, reasonable voices, 'We must get some decent cricket.' St Benedict asked of the novice that he should truly seek God, that he be prepared to live in obedience, that he should face difficulties or 'opprobrium' and that he should live in the Praise of God. If Cardinal Hume found all that difficult at eighteen, he adjusted remarkably well to life at the monastery and school on the Yorkshire moors. He taught French and theology, he coached the rugby team, he was sent to a university in Switzerland where he studied Aquinas who taught him that a belief in God could be obtained by reason alone, and he became a tolerant housemaster who told his boys with unanswerable logic: 'I don't mind you making a noise if you don't mind me stopping you.'

'Did you have crises of faith?'

'I don't know about crises. Difficulties.'

'What difficulties?'

'Well, the problem of evil in the world . . . and the existence of other religions.'

'The problem of evil?' I asked. 'I mean, you have to believe in a God who could permit the massacre of millions of Jews?'

'There are problems.' The Cardinal frowned. 'That and worshippers in church, killed in the Italian earthquake.'

I asked him about children crushed to death in crowds that went to see the Pope: of a child I had loved, killed by aimless chance running for the school bus. I hoped I wouldn't be offered an easy answer about God gathering his favourites to himself and, of course, I wasn't.

'In this world I can't understand it. But that doesn't affect my belief. I believe we're a fallen race, that human life is always in the hands of fallen people, and when I'm faced with the ghastliness of concentration camps and so on, I can't put it to God at my level. This is a very monk-like way of putting it, but I believe we should be on a pilgrimage in search of the truth. Full understanding is never possible. The faith is in seeking understanding, that's what St Anselm said. *Your* saint.'

'But if we can't be content with not understanding?' I felt inclined to deny my proprietary interest in St Anselm.

'Then we always have the free choice of Non-God. But that's a choice for frustrated isolation.'

He was smiling, but I felt a small shiver, recognizing the faith I had taken on, the lonely dedication of the atheist.

'We necessarily only have a small and limited understanding. But we must keep moving on. That's the pilgrimage. The finding is in the seeking.'

'What have you found? I mean, you've been seeking for a good many years.'

'What have I found?' The cardinal took a long time to consider. 'I suppose a simpler faith. Deeper. Of course, it isn't all a cloud of unknowing. God has revealed himself by becoming man.'

'Did you ever have a mystic experience of God, when you were a monk?'

'Some people may have had. I didn't.'

'What do you feel, when you pray?'

'Oh, I just keep plugging away. At its best it's like being in a dark room with someone you love. You can't see them; but you know they're there.'

'And about birth control . . .' The tea was getting cold. I had eaten all the cake and we both turned to the question with a sort of weariness.

'Journalists always have to ask that.'

'I'm sorry. But there is a fair amount of interest in sex?'

'I don't think our role is to be the custodians of sex.' The celibate cardinal showed a modesty rare in Catholic prelates. 'I think sex looms too large in people's thoughts about Catholicism. After all, we have far more interesting things to talk about.' Having just bought, in Westminster Cathedral, a papal discourse to an organization of midwives, I could only agree. 'But I think natural family planning should include self-denial,' he said.

'Is self-denial good for the soul?'

'I think so. I had a married couple in here who told me that every time they had sex without using the pill it was like going on another honeymoon.'

Reflecting on the enormously varied satisfactions that can be obtained from married life, I led the conversation back to the subject of death.

'Do you believe in heaven?'

'If death were the end then life's absurd.'

'Well, exactly,' I agreed. The cardinal was touching on one of my most closely held beliefs.

'I can't think that life, after such aspirations, ends up in the absurd. That *would* make it nasty, brutish and short.'

'In a television film I've seen about you you're shown visiting an old woman dying of cancer. You tell her she'll see God very soon. Did you mean that, literally?'

'You must use simple expressions to simple people.'

'And hell?'

'That's the choice of Non-God. That's isolation.'

'Do you enjoy this job?'

'It's fascinating. Of course, you never have time to do all you should. But it's marvellous to talk to so many people. I've never been a priest, you see; it's remarkable how many people you can help by saying something quite simple.'

'Do you see yourself,' I asked him, offering him the choice between the great political church figurehead, the brilliant Ecclesiastic of the World, and the lonely poet and dreamer, 'as Cardinal Manning or Cardinal Newman?'

'That's an interesting one.' Today's cardinal looked at the clock. 'I think I'd rather not answer.'

But what is he? With his gentleness, his reluctance, according to his Ampleforth colleagues, to take hurtful decisions, he is perhaps, for all his television fame and political expertise, a Newman in Manning's clothing.

★

In the upper reaches of Archbishop's House, Cardinal Hume has his own quarters, the housemaster's room where he listens to Haydn on his record player and has his books, among them Kenneth Clark on civilization, Edward Heath on sailing, his picture of Chris Evert and his notice which says, 'It's lonely at the top.' It's the room of a games-playing, celibate ex-schoolmaster who has said, 'It must be marvellous to have a wife.' As he took me down to the entrance of the great gloomy ecclesiastical station hotel he said, 'What I always say is, "Stick to St Peter's boat. When the sea's rough and the weather's rocky, stick to the boat of St Peter. Depend on the Pope." '

'Shall I see Mr Mortimer out, father?' his chaplain offered. But the cardinal took me all the way to his front door, saying that the exercise was good for him.

'And tomorrow?' I asked him as we parted. 'Do you get up very early?'

'Much later than in the monastery. I get up around six o'clock, as a matter of fact.'

'I get up at six also.'

'Then that proves,' Cardinal Hume looked at me and scored his final point, 'that you are a natural monastic.'

Portrait of the Artist as a Naughty Boy

DAVID HOCKNEY

'As I grow older the glasses get smaller. Of course, I'm still blond. I've been blond for twenty-three years. My mother thinks it's natural.'

In fact David Hockney, at forty-three, has changed little. His is still the dry, comical voice of everyone's favourite North Country auntie. He wears small gold granny glasses instead of the big horn-rimmed, pop-period gig lamps, his features are sharper, he is thinner and stoops slightly; but moving round his studio hung with some new paintings ('I did them to cover the wall. For my own amusement. If you do things for your own amusement other people often like them too') he became younger by the minute, until the time when he switched on the lights and rang up the curtain in his model theatre, and changed the enchanting scenery for his New York Metropolitan production of a triple bill of the ballet *Parade* and two short operas *Les Mamelles du Tirésias* and *L'Enfant et les sortilèges*. And then he waltzed, wearing his dark-blue baseball cap and yellow T-shirt and voluminous grey-flannel trousers, to the music of Maurice Ravel.

'My father was an eccentric,' said Mr Hockney. 'He worked for twenty-five years as an audit clerk in Bradford; but he was always making things. He made prams. Not very good prams. And he did posters – for CND and the Bradford Diabetics. At Christmas he stuck tinsel on his posters, which they all thought was rather vulgar.'

David Hockney has a portrait drawing by his father grandly entitled 'Bertrand Russell. Peace Campaigner' which he managed to get into a corner of one of his own exhibitions in the Hayward Gallery. Once Hockney *père* set out by train for the Aldermaston March and in charge of all the Nuclear Disarmament banners, some of his own making: unhappily he fell asleep before Reading and was carried on to South Wales with his banners, where he became involved in a violent argument about the fare.

'My father thought of Russia as a land of cornfields and happy laughter, and he used to drop copies of the *Daily Worker* around casually for people to read. Mother was always hissing at him and telling him to pick them up.

'My father took some art lessons and when the Leonardo cartoon was in the news, Dad said, "I know what that's called. It's called 'Light and Shade'." They taught him light and shade from that picture at his class; they don't teach it any more, although, as a matter of fact, light and shade are still there.'

Keen on light and shade himself, David Hockney has a respect for conventional art teaching; by the age of sixteen he had committed himself to Bradford Art School and spent four days a week learning to draw, lessons which can rarely have been put to better use, the line in a Hockney drawing, as in a Picasso, being never less than superbly confident and always truthful.

'Drawing's important. It's about looking. That's what drawing does,' he says. 'It teaches you how to look.'

'Can you teach drawing?'

'You can teach some things about it. The poetry you can't teach.'

'You enjoyed the Royal College?'

'It was a good time, with Allen Jones and Ralph Koltai. At Bradford I'd never seen Cubism – all we saw were the Euston Road Group. I sold a drawing to another student for £10 and went to Paris: on the way home I had enough money for a bed for the night or the duty-free cigarettes. I bought the cigarettes and slept in a doorway.'

Before he went on to the Royal College, David Hockney did his two years' National Service in the skin ward of Bradford hospital. He used to paint old men with various coloured ointments '('Don't forget the testicles, David'), give them blue and yellow arms and legs and gentian violet behinds. He would run to the street corner and place their bets for them, and wash them and lay out their dead bodies when they itched no more.

'You get used to corpses. It's terrible how you get used to them. I remember one old man with an appalling skin complaint; he used to go into the ointment room and get painted all the colours of the rainbow. Finally they threw him out because he wouldn't have his teeth extracted. Six weeks later I met him in the street; and he was completely cured, with skin like a baby. He'd met a woman boiling herbs in Bradford Market. He drank up the water and it cured him. I entirely believe it.

'All bodies are beautiful. Of course, some are younger or more sensuous than others, but it would be terrible to say anyone's body's not beautiful. It would be horrible to say it. My mother's body's beautiful. Everyone's is. Of course, in England they think getting pleasure from a visual experience is a kind of sin.'

'Do you think we're very puritanical?'

'Puritanical! Mrs Whitehouse must have a deep hatred of art. Didn't she just get a knighthood or something?'

'Something like that, yes.'

'If I lived in England now I'd get really political. I'd take up some cause. Like the horrible business of these violinists down the Underground.'

Mr Hockney is a thorough newspaper reader. He read this week of a party of buskers apparently arrested and dragged off by the police for playing their violins in the Underground, an act of brute bureaucracy which shamefully caused no riots among the cowed citizenry on the Bakerloo Line.

'If I was living here I'd organize orchestras, and get them to fill the Underground with music.'

'You see,' I tried to find an explanation for this grizzly event, 'the London Commissioner for Police is a Scot.'

'That's it!' Mr Hockney was drinking Guinness from a bottle

and looking profoundly depressed. 'We ought to give home rule to Wales and Scotland and then we could have Merry England once again. You know what I'd organize if I lived in England? "The Piss-Off Society." That's what I'd tell all these planners and obnoxious people who tried to control us. Things are healthier in America, you can land in Los Angeles and get all the sex you want on your Master Card.

'I even got inhibited painting in England. I found I was beginning to paint very tightly and deliberately.' Mr Hockney stood in a tight and bureaucratic huddle, his arms close to his sides. 'Now I've started painting much more freely, and faster. I think it's working in the theatre that did it. You know what the Glyndebourne scene-painters said about my *The Magic Flute*? They said they had to wear sunglasses to paint it.'

No one who has seen the Hockney *Magic Flute* with its apparently simple but magical and profound designs will regret his new enthusiasm for working in opera. 'It took six months just to make the models. I'm an original painter, I suppose; so I don't mind being an underpaid designer.'

David Hockney wandered round his studio, and showed his treasures: the volumes of his photographs, going back to his first visit to America, and the days before he went blond, and his gadgets, a miniature camera, and a small cassette player with light headphones and surprising powers of reproduction. 'It's a Japanese machine that plays Italian opera, which is more satisfactory than an Italian machine that plays Japanese opera . . .' So he sits in the National Gallery, silently listening to Rossini in front of Longhi's paintings of Venice or snapping corners of the Rokeby Venus with the tiny camera concealed under the long peak of his baseball cap. If any attendant protests, he resorts, although gently, to 'Piss-Off' politics.

'Of course you should be allowed to photograph pictures. They only stop people to boost their sale of postcards. In one gallery they actually had a notice which said "No Sketching". How obnoxious! I said, "How do you think these things got on the walls if there was no sketching?" '

'Do you know the story of the *L'Enfant et les sortilèges*? It's by Colette. There's this little boy and his mother says, "You can only have tea and no sugar till you've done your homework." So he misbehaves. He tears up a book and pulls the squirrel's tail and attacks the wallpaper and dances on a chair and says, "I want to be wicked. Wicked!" And then everything turns on him. A flame comes out of the fire at him and the wallpaper attacks him and so does the chair, and the teapot sings in English. They all sing, "Wretched boy," and the princess comes out of the book and sings, "Wretched boy, since you tore my book no one will ever know how my story ended." But finally they sing, "Wretched boy, perhaps he's not so bad after all." I like the story very much. I can understand that, an excited, naughty child. If *he* gets forgiven, perhaps there's hope for all of us.'

David Hockney, who at least took enough liberties as an excited boy to have the furniture dance for him, has had a career which after an uncertain and 'deliberately childish' start, according to his teachers at the Royal College, has been remarkably and consistently successful.

'At least I can say one thing. I've managed to live an artist all my life. It's been a privilege.'

It's a privilege, also, to have him with us. We should do something to keep him, even if it means sending a load of violinists down the Tube.

The Guru and the Radioactive Frog

E. P. THOMPSON

'If you saw a frog jumping about, you would have to wash it down to get rid of active dust, cook and eat it.' So said the vice-chairman of Civil Aid, advising possible survivors of a nuclear holocaust, according to *The Times* in February this year.

In all the vast quantity of words that have been written on the subject of nuclear arms, there can be no description so depressing as that of the few survivors of a blasted England hungrily chasing radioactive frogs, as selected civil servants and high-ranking police officers emerge from burrows to impose martial law, and Mrs Thatcher and her merry men, from their top-secret bunker in the Home Counties, put a further squeeze on the non-existent economy.

The fact that this prospect can be contemplated by such, no doubt, intelligent people as the vice-chairman of Civil Aid, and government ministers, is undoubtedly what has caused the biggest boost for the Campaign for Nuclear Disarmament since J. B. Priestley and Canon Collins marched from Aldermaston, and Bertrand Russell and Robert Bolt sat down in Trafalgar Square. The old, comforting idea was that we could all live happily under the protection of a nicely adjusted balance of terror. Now that Britain has opted for the Cruise missile the protection seems thinner than ever. The CND has doubled its membership and formed 200 new groups in a year. The organization estimates that a quarter of a million people turned out for a Sunday rally in

Trafalgar Square. A huge assortment of young, middle-aged and elderly people, with no one political affiliation, are beginning to wonder if by far the best form of nuclear defence might be no nuclear defence at all.

The guru, the inspirer and by far the most eloquent advocate of this movement is the one-time reader in social history at Warwick University and the author of *The Making of the English Working Class*, E. P. Thompson.

'Talk about myself? I'm not sure I like that.'

We sat together, Mr Thompson and I, two ageing radicals, in the Savoy Grill, which early in the evening looked like the first-class dining room after the *Titanic* had hit a floating depression.

'Start at the beginning.'

'My father was a Methodist and a poet. He was an educational missionary padre in India. He became a friend of the Bengali poet Rabindranath Tagore, and of Nehru. Then he came home to Oxford where he wrote poetry and got a small job as a research fellow. He always said he'd been wrong to try and convert the Bengalis to Christianity when they had a perfectly satisfactory religion of their own.'

At fifty-six, E. P. Thompson is a white-haired, remarkably handsome man who looks like a modest but successful actor with bohemian tastes. He was wearing a comfortable old tweed jacket with a CND badge, and ordered turbot as though it were some strange delicacy which he had rarely seen.

'My mother was a missionary too. An American missionary to the Lebanon. Oh God,' he said as I wrote it down. 'I can see what you're going to make of that!'

'Schools?'

'I went to a prep school in Oxford.'

My memory lurched and came into focus, I saw a nine-year-old Edward Palmer Thompson, his socks round his ankles, rushing after a ball while I cowered and shivered miserably somewhere near the touch-line.

'I know,' he sighed. 'We were at the Dragon School together. I was a scruffy child: rather good at rugger. Please let's forget all about that. I went on to Kingswood, the Methodist school. I wrote poetry there and became a kind of Walt Whitman pantheist. I was a Communist by the time I was sixteen. It was anti-Fascism that made me join the party.'

'You didn't leave it until 1956?'

'I didn't leave the Communist Party,' the ex-reader in social history smiled gently and sampled the Sauvignon. 'The Communist Party left me. Of course, I'd always been in the opposition in the party. We started the *New Reasoner* and tried to be critical. The British Communist Party is in the impossible position of trying to follow a formula evolved for a foreign people. A lot of countries had that trouble in the nineteenth century when they tried to imitate the French Revolution.'

'And during the war?'

'Oh, I fought. The last war was very necessary. I was in tanks.'

'And you killed people?'

'Oh yes.' He talked softly and ate slowly and not very much. 'Yes. I expect so.'

'Now that nuclear weapons exist, you have to face the fact that you would rather be conquered by, say, the Russians than have the world blown up?'

'Yes, I think so. Don't you?'

'Better red than dead?'

'Yes.'

'So, if nuclear weapons had existed in 1939, we would have had to accept conquest by Hitler to save a nuclear war?'

There was only a slight pause as the disarmer faced the final consequences of his argument. Then he said, 'Yes.'

At Warwick, E. P. Thompson sympathized deeply with the students who protested at their lack of representation on any important policy-making committee and who wished to see the secret reports which apparently existed on some members of the university. No doubt he was out of sympathy with a seat of learning which boasts the "Barclays Bank Professor of Management Information Systems' and the 'Volkswagen Professor of German'. E. P.

Thompson also found himself confronted by Warwick's chancellor, Lord Radcliffe, whose Report on Security Procedures in the Public Service contained the immortal line, infuriating to anyone who grew up in the emotional atmosphere of the Spanish Civil War, 'For the sake of brevity we have used the phrase "communist" throughout to include fascists.'

Indeed Lord Radcliffe, about whom Mr Thompson has written with a good deal of grudging respect, seems the eternal enemy. Radcliffe was a Lord of Appeal, a natural member of the ruling classes, urbane, civilized and conservative. He it was who worked out the division of India, and wrote in glowing terms of the long-dead administrations of the British Raj and Rudyard Kipling. But E. P. Thompson is also part of our imperial past, the son of the missionary who knew Nehru and Tagore. His radical views are very English, a mixture of genuine sympathy for a historically exploited working class and a confident feeling of intellectual superiority to almost anyone likely to form a government.

'Jury vetting!' E. P. Thompson spoke about a subject which, like the recent secrets trial, he has written about with pungent disdain. 'What are you lawyers doing about jury vetting?'

'Nothing much. No one's doing much about the death of Habeas Corpus either.'

He looked at me as though that was to be expected from Lord Radcliffe's profession, and pushed away his plate of turbot half-eaten.

'Do you think this is the period with least concern for individual liberty we've lived through?' I meant, but didn't dare to add, 'Since we were at the Dragon School together.'

'I think so. I think we're shuffling into authoritarianism. I can't imagine anyone in Gladstone's day saying they approved of jury-vetting. But,' Mr Thompson admitted, 'I can imagine it going on.'

'Do you think this government's really concerned about freedom?'

'Doesn't it all look marvellous?' The arrival of the sweet trolley produced a charming smile from the nuclear disarmer, and an order for trifle. The Savoy Grill was filling up, the well-spaced tables became populated with quiet customers apparently unaware of the fact that they might soon be ordering radioactive frog.

'You're very pessimistic, aren't you?' I asked him. 'You're sure there will be a war.'

'It needs so little. For instance, there's an appalling régime in Pakistan. The people might revolt and the revolutionary government would turn to Russia. Then, if the Americans panic . . .' He sat, sunk in thought, and then said, 'I was very pessimistic until the CND rally in Trafalgar Square last Sunday. Now I feel much more cheerful.'

'Is the problem just Cruise missiles?'

'Not really. In fact, Cruise missiles are the least of our worries, although we have decided to allow a foreign power to use parts of our country as advanced bomb sites. In theory, a Cruise missile in East Anglia could reach Moscow, whereas a Russian SS 20 can get nowhere near the USA. So you can imagine that the Russians feel threatened by these weapons in England, all under American control. But no one knows if Cruise missiles will work, and they have a 50 per cent failure rate in test flights. The first one that goes off will probably take out Massachusetts.

'The point is that, by having nuclear weapons, we make Britain the prime target for attack. Michael Howard, the Regius Professor of History at Oxford, admitted that in his letter to *The Times* when he wrote, "The presence of Cruise missiles on British soil makes it highly possible that this country would be the target for a series of preemptive strikes by Soviet missiles." '

'So what's the answer?'

'They're doing rather well in Europe. In spite of the NATO resolution, the Dutch have refused to have Cruise and the Belgians, and the Danes, and the Norwegians have made it clear from the outset that they want nothing to do with them. I don't know why we can't join the sensible countries.'

'Is it really going to make a difference?'

'If Europe's a non-nuclear zone? I think it will. Look, the real point is the terrible East–West division in Europe. It's breaking down already. We're growing closer in a way, not further apart. Poland is in hock to Western capital. Young Czechs listen to rock music and they're so resistant to their government that they tell you Allende was a Fascist leader in Chile just because they never believe the official party line. So at least we could make a start, and lower the tensions in Europe . . .'

'Where's the CND been all these years?' I asked, remembering the long period of silence from the disarmers.

'The world changed. And protests changed too. The object of the protesters became the American intervention in Vietnam, and the protest was not pacifist but aggressive.'

'And what's brought it back to life?'

'A lot of things. The growing isolation of America. The NATO resolution to allow Cruise missiles. The fear of nuclear disasters at Three Mile Island and so on. It's brought it all back.'

'Just as it was?'

'As peaceful as it was. On Sunday what you saw was an old type of demonstration. Without aggro. And people of all ages.'

'A demonstration of pacifists?'

'Not all pacifists. I'm not a pacifist. If I were a Yugoslav I'd certainly fight if my country were invaded by Russia.'

'But not with nuclear weapons?'

'Exactly.'

When the atom bomb fell, there were long cheers from the men in E. P. Thompson's regiment because they wouldn't have to go and fight in the East. Only he and a friend were silent; and he didn't know the full horror of his deliverance until John Hersey wrote *Hiroshima* in 1950. Not only did 140,000 people perish in the explosion in Hiroshima and 70,000 in Nagasaki, but tens of thousands died later of various cancers and other diseases, and clearly these bombs were of insignificant power compared to modern nuclear weapons.

Mr Thompson quotes no less an authority than Lord Louis Mountbatten who said, shortly before he was murdered: 'In the event of a nuclear war there will be no chances, there will be no survivors, all will be obliterated.'

The day before I met E. P. Thompson, I heard Mr Francis Pym on the radio say that, of course, we all agreed with the aims of CND, but just for the moment, just until something could be organized, Cruise missiles and nuclear submarines were necessary for the 'preservation of democracy'. Mr Pym has also said, 'From the point of view of siting the Cruise missiles I don't think it makes a great deal of difference. It is really a security and defence and strategic consideration, and of course one must take public opinion into account as far as one possibly can.'

Public opinion came out, E. P. Thompson thinks, in Trafalgar Square one Sunday, but neither Mr Pym, nor his colleagues in the government, seemed prepared to take any particular account of it.

We had finished dinner. Mr Thompson collected his carrier bag full of belongings and we walked out into the wet Strand.

'You know, I could have talked quite well to you, if you hadn't been taking notes.'

'I'm sorry. Look,' I asked him, 'suppose that meeting in Trafalgar Square doesn't achieve anything?'

'That's not really the point, is it? The point is, it shows that democracy's alive. People aren't just prepared to accept what the politicians tell them. A rally like that gives us self-respect. Chartism was terribly good for the Chartists although they never got the Charter.'

And then he dived off into the traffic. I went home, as we have all done every night since the world began, with the hourly possibility of death, disease and disaster and the blotting out of the world. Is it all different now? Are we faced with an entirely new terror? I felt slightly guilty, perhaps, at being insufficiently afraid.

The Elegant Brick Dropper

SIR JOHN GIELGUD

His back is straight, his head cocked, the nose is like an eager beak cleaving the air, the eyes are hooded as if prepared to wince in fastidious disapproval at what that over-inquisitive nose might sniff. He has the bald head of a priest, the pink health of a retired admiral, the elegant suiting of what was once known as a 'man about town' and the competent hands of an artist. After playing most of the great tragic heroes in his youth, John Gielgud has developed, in his seventies, into the world's subtlest comic actor. This may be less of a change than it seems. I remember him saying that it was his comic training, learnt partly from his intense admiration for Noël Coward, which taught him to play Hamlet, and to find the comedy which is always near to the still heart of Lear.

I had lunch with John Gielgud in the canteen at Thames Television. He ordered a bottle of red wine and a steak and talked incessantly, an outpouring of uninhibited, apparently happy memories, gossip and plans with hardly a pause for breath. His eyes turned to gaze round the room as though, through modesty, not taking part in the conversation. His hands moved rhythmically. 'Tynan said I had only two gestures, the left hand up, the right hand up – what did he want me to do, bring out my prick?' The word is swallowed, the talk sweeps on. 'Edith Evans was savage as Lady Bracknell. You see, she came from a family of servants whom the Lady Bracknells of this world rang for to put a lump of coal on the fire. Her performance was pure revenge.' 'Gerald du Maurier was marvellous in scenes with young girls. He was able to stand away from them and express such erotic tenderness.' 'Don't write about my successes, the failures are much more interesting.' 'Agate came round to my dressing room in the interval of the first night of *Macbeth* and said, "I've come to congratulate you now; by the end of the performance I'll probably have changed my mind!" ' 'Agate did behave dreadfully, Marie Tempest had to tick him off for it.' 'I can't imagine what they thought at the Royal Court when I arrived in my Rolls and Ralph Richardson thundered up on his huge motor-bike! Backstage was full of old cigarette packets and young men in pigtails, but so kind, and they couldn't have worked harder at the Haymarket.'

'When Peter Sellers went on television and said I'd made that awful remark about another actor, you know, the one who had, I said, a face like cold veal, I lay awake all night worrying and then thank God I discovered it was Coral Browne who'd said it and not me.' 'I did enjoy doing your play although my agent told me not to. I've never known agents who tried to stop you working before.'

'My eyes are so horribly good.' They were, indeed, looking far away, making careful notes on the costumes of a group of actors leaving the canteen. 'I can see almost everyone in the stalls. My performance almost collapsed one night when I saw Noël Coward didn't come back after the interval.' 'I always saw Romeo and Macbeth as characters, but I found it terribly difficult to get away from the idea that Hamlet was me. It was enormous effort to act the part technically and not just be it.' 'Gerald du Maurier really was tactless. He was deputed by the committee of the Garrick Club to tell a well-known director he'd been black-balled. The director looked very unhappy and finally he asked, trying to make the best of it, "Were there many black-balls?" "My dear fellow," du Maurier said, "have you ever seen sheep shit?" '

I sat entranced, almost silent, and remembered that Gielgud once had lunch with a writer called Edward Knoblock. 'Do you see that man coming in?' Gielgud said to Knoblock in one of those glorious, totally unmalicious boobs which happen when the rushing stream of his thoughts breaks its banks, 'He's the biggest bore in London – second only to Edward Knoblock.' And then, in a terrible attempt to put matters right, he added hopelessly, 'Not you, of course. I mean the *other* Edward Knoblock.'

In the 1930s my father and I used to climb into dinner jackets and winged collars to visit the theatre. I was, at the age of ten, dressed like a waiter, unbearably precocious; but the excitement as the curtain trembled and rose on a white throne room and on the young Gielgud as King Richard of Bordeaux, whose golden sleeves swept the ground, was genuine and unforgettable. I can also see now, in a set the colour of autumn, that 1934 Hamlet which Sir John had such difficulty in remembering was not him: and which I, at twelve, and I'm sure everyone else in the audience, clearly knew to be themselves. I had cherished his photograph, the clear features of the matinée idol, wearing a snap-brimmed trilby and a light grey suit, as that *jeune premier* which every great seventy-year-old actor has to have somewhere in his past.

Lunch with Sir John does not only bring back what, to some, may seem the vanishing magic of the pre-war West End, but also the Victorian theatre aristocracy of which Gielgud was a child. His grandmother, Kate Terry, played Ophelia, Juliet, Beatrice and Portia before settling down in a large house on Campden Hill with Arthur Lewis, a fashionable haberdasher who organized evenings with a Glee Club and kept a cow for fresh milk somewhere near Holland Avenue. Kate was the eldest of the family of Terrys which included Fred, who created the Scarlet Pimpernel and went on playing that role though crippled with gout, Marion, who played the shady Mrs Erlynne in *Lady Windermere's Fan*, and, above all, Ellen. Gielgud remembers Ellen Terry as an old lady, swathed in shawls and crowned with a huge black hat, unable to recollect lines or which was which among her vast crowd of nephews and nieces. She beckoned the young John to her and said, 'Which are you and do you read your Shakespeare?'

All the Terrys had the same weakness. 'Poor lachrymal glands, my dear,' a famous specialist told Gielgud's mother, who cried gently but almost incessantly like a wet April. Ellen Terry knew that her tears impressed some of her audience, but she found them a nuisance and had to work hard to stop the flow. Phyllis Neilson-

Terry, Gielgud's cousin, used to contemplate a theatre and say, 'Shall we give them *real* tears tonight?' Gielgud finds that genuine weeping impresses the actor more than the spectator, but he does cry with great expertise without, he says, 'as in real life, choking or running at the nose'. In this sentence, it seems to me, lies much of the secret of the great actor's art. The audience is moved by his tears, which are perfectly genuine; although they are shed with sufficient care to prevent running at the nose.

Gielgud's grand Terry relatives taught him that he must always call a job 'an engagement' and never speak of his salary until he was made an offer. His first professional engagement came at the age of seventeen when he walked on to the stage of the Old Vic as the herald in *Henry V*, whose one and only line is, 'Here is the number of the slaughtered French.' It seems that the delivery of this somewhat lugubrious statement was so poor that for the rest of the season, although he walked on in *King Lear* and *Peer Gynt*, he was given no line at all.

Two years later, after a spell at RADA, Nigel Playfair gave Gielgud the part of Felix the Butterfly in Čapek's *The Insect Play*. In this role, Sir John recalls in his autobiography, *Early Stages*, 'I made an extremely bad impression. I wore white flannels, a silk shirt, a green laurel wreath, fair hair and carried a golden battledore and shuttlecock. I am surprised that the audience didn't throw things at me.'

He had always moved awkwardly. Lady Benson, his first drama teacher, burst out laughing when she saw him and said he walked exactly like a cat with rickets: not exactly an encouragement to a teenage actor who knew that, while his voice would always soar into interesting cadences and frequently move him to tears, his legs simply refused to obey his instructions.

When he did his first Romeo, Ivor Brown woundingly wrote, 'Mr Gielgud from the waist downwards means absolutely nothing.' It is typical of his modesty that Gielgud himself said that he acted as if his knees were tied together with ribbons. No doubt if he had spent more time on the playing fields of Westminster, and less shining electric torches on the cutouts and tinsel of his toy theatre, he might have been in greater command of his wayward legs. From the start he was a voice, an intellect and a pair of expressive shoulders moved to grief or, as easily, shaken by laughter. And, when it came to it, no doubt Hamlet was not much good at football either.

After the disaster of *The Insect Play*, Gielgud went to the Oxford Playhouse – a weekly rep run in a draughty hall by J. B. Fagan, a disciple of Granville Barker who was beginning to introduce Chekhov, Ibsen and Pirandello to a sometimes sparse but always enthusiastic North Oxford audience.

By the age of twenty his training was finished. And then came the chance to understudy Noël Coward in *The Vortex* and take over from him in that play and *The Constant Nymph*. Gielgud learnt his impeccable comic timing from Coward, and became a star when Lilian Baylis asked him to go to the Old Vic in 1929 and play the great Shakespearian roles at the rate of one every four weeks. In *Richard II* and then in his first *Hamlet*, Gielgud captivated the difficult but enthusiastic Old Vic audience. His voice ensnared and enslaved them, no one had ever spoken Shakespeare with such intelligence and understanding, they cried when Richard was deposed and Hamlet was carried to the battlements. No one ever mentioned a cat with rickets again.

Shakespeare had not been played in the West End since the days of Irving and Tree – but Gielgud made him a box-office triumph in Shaftesbury Avenue and on Broadway. He was the golden boy to whom success came early (later, at the end of the war, he was to look over his list of ambitions and find, much to his disappointment, that he had achieved them all). So I sat at lunch with the bald, rubicund old soldier-priest and had no difficulty in imagining the endlessly chattering, rather too well-dressed young actor of the 1930s against whom, at first sight, the young Ralph Richardson had taken so strongly. 'I found his clothes extravagant,' Richardson has said. 'I found his conversation flippant. I didn't like him. But, when I played Caliban to his Prospero, John said to me one day, "Would you care to run over your scene with me?" I thought to myself, "Not much." But we ran it through and he gave me about two hundred ideas as he usually does and I thought, "My God, I might do one of those." And when I went away, I thought, "This chap, you know, I don't like him very much but by God he knows something about this here play." Out of that we formed a firm friendship. We used to go out to lunch together. I was always rather amazed at him – a kind of brilliant butterfly, while I was a very gloomy sort of boy.'

'I have three besetting sins, both on and off the stage,' Gielgud wrote at the end of *Early Stages*, '– impetuosity, selfconsciousness and a lack of interest in anything not immediately concerned with myself or with the theatre.'

You can take it from this that Gielgud is not a political animal. It is also true that many of the more tedious facts of the outside world seem to have escaped his notice. Walking home from the theatre one night during the Blitz, he happened to glance up at the moonlit barrage balloons. 'Oh dear,' he murmured to his companion, 'our poor boys must be terribly lonely up there.'

I remember going to dinner in a house where Gielgud was a guest. Our daughter was very young and we brought her with us and put her to sleep in a spare bedroom. As we slunk downstairs with the carry-cot he looked cautiously into the pink plastic container.

'Why on earth do you bring your baby with you?' He seemed genuinely puzzled. 'Is it because you're afraid of burglars?'

Not that the world does not touch him, as it does all of us. During Alan Bennett's *Forty Years On*, in which he played a headmaster, he would leave the stage each night with a line adlibbed to one of the schoolboys, such as, 'So glad Green House did so well in the swimming cup, Jenkins,' or, 'Got to beat Swains in the cross-country, haven't we, Jenkins?' One night he went off saying sadly, 'Jenkins, I have got the most terrible problems with my income tax.'

In 1950 Gielgud was asked to lead the Stratford Company. He was forty-six and the latest Shakespearian triumphs had been scored by Olivier and Richardson with the Old Vic Company at the New. He was to play Angelo in *Measure for Measure*, directed by the twenty-five-year-old Peter Brook. It is an unglamorous role and Brook was determined that it should be played with severity and truth.

Gielgud wore a close-fitting black cap instead of the blond wig he had chosen first. He hardly moved when he first saw Isabella: but his whole body tensed as if at the impact of an extraordinary intellectual electric shock. The day of the *jeune premier* was well over; but England had a great classical actor at the very height of his powers.

England did not show itself particularly grateful. In the next decade the theatre changed enormously: the typical matinée idol acquired a roll-neck sweater and a North Country accent. Gielgud made what he acknowledges to be a mistake in reacting in a somewhat mandarin fashion to the new writing of the 1960s. With unforgiveable stupidity the theatre responded by neglecting him and he sank into something that, to the amazement and distress of his friends, seemed very like gloom.

He worked hard as a director, changing his mind, talking incessantly, firing off – as he had done at Ralph Richardson all those years ago – 250 ideas a minute, trying to stop Richard Burton playing Hamlet like a Welsh rugger forward. ('We'll go to dinner when you're ready,' was what Gielgud honestly meant to say to Burton in the dressing room: but that loquacious subconscious rushed into the open with, 'We'll go to dinner when you're better.') But, it seemed, sadly, that the days of the great performances were over.

All occasions, as Gielgud's Hamlet said, seemed to inform against him. He wanted to do King Lear again, but Paul Scofield's great success in Peter Brook's production made that difficult. Brecht came into fashion and his style dictated the Shakespeare productions of the early 1960s; and leading actors like David Warner and Ian Holm were offering a new line in classless kings and princes from a red-brick Elsinore. Dramatists chose determinedly working-class settings and Gielgud would no doubt have been and looked miserable on a Joan Littlewood building site, or in a Wesker kitchen. Not only was he not invited to contribute to the 400th

Shakespeare anniversary in 1964; no 'new' writer offered a play to him.

Happily, fashions in the theatre pass quickly and no great actor can long stay unemployed. Tony Richardson found in Gielgud a miraculously polished and comic film actor. Peter Brook directed him in Seneca's *Oedipus* at the National Theatre and did it, he said, 'as a real homage to John'. He acted like a painting by Francis Bacon, his body splayed and twisted: his legs by now having learnt implicit obedience. Peace between Gielgud and the new dramatists was signed when his Rolls and Richardson's motor-bike purred up to the Court for the rehearsals of David Storey's play, *Home*.

When we met, Gielgud was sharing a Westminster house, elegant as a set for a comedy of manners, with a friend who is so devoted to animals that large birds flap about, making the basement, it seems, a little too like the grandfather's attic in Ibsen's *The Wild Duck*. They were about to move to a large house in Buckinghamshire. John Gielgud looked to the future in his seventies, excited, undismayed, chattering endlessly. In a profession which thrives on malice, no one has ever suggested that his splendid gaffes are deliberate; no one speaks of him without affection.

'I enjoyed our lunch,' he told me. Not because of anything I said but because, I believe, he enjoyed the life we were discussing so much. From the day when he raised the curtain on his home-made model theatre, with scenery painted under the influence of his cousin Gordon Craig, for a scene he had written depicting that ex-Ophelia, his grandmother, Kate Terry, on board ship in the throes of sea sickness, shouting fruitlessly for her deaf maid, his life promised Gielgud a great deal. Since then it has kept its promise, to him and to us.

Brother Ken and Sister Chair

KEN LIVINGSTONE

'For the first time we've got an army trained to subdue a civil population, and the whole of the serious left could be executed in half a day. Who knows what's going to happen in a year or two? We could have a radical Socialist government under attack from the army or the police like in Spain or Chile. Or it might be threatened by the banks. That's one of the reasons why the police must be answerable to us.'

I had this sudden vision of Mr Eric Heffer being led blindfold to the wall or the Commissioner of Police forming an unholy alliance with the NatWest to take over the BBC. For this radical talk was going on, not in a smoke-filled backroom in Bogotá or Madrid, but over a cup of tea in London's County Hall, that home of gently humming bureaucracy in which nothing more disturbing used to be heard than the clink of mayoral chains at civic receptions, the chatter of aldermen and their good ladies, and the mutter of devoted members of the Inner London Education Authority as they padded down panelled corridors still vaguely impregnated with the smell of the late Herbert Morrison's pipe.

I was taking tea with Kenneth Livingstone who, after eight hard-working and anonymous years of, as he says, 'slowly undermining my elders and betters', has arrived to be perhaps the first genuinely left-wing leader to achieve real power in England. He has entered into his kingdom long before his mentor Tony Benn, so he is the forerunner as well as the disciple, the Huxley to Benn's Darwin, the John the Baptist to Benn's . . . but the comparisons should go no further. It's enough to say that a close study of Ken might give you some flavour of life with Tony.

'We've got to control the police,' Ken Livingstone went on, 'because if they are allowed to get hold of water cannon and plastic bullets it'll only mean that both sides may escalate to guns. We've got to be able to change police procedure and then we might even stop them breaking up "front-line" Brixton houses with sledgehammers.'

'Don't you think you might have made things worse by going down to Brixton after the riots and criticizing the police?'

'Someone has to say these things; they don't get said in the gutter press. I happened to be in Brixton because I went to an Anti-Nazi League meeting that had been organized for months. It was extraordinary there at that time. The streets were silent, there were no cars or buses. It was like a war zone.'

Whether or not there is a revolution threatening in the streets, Livingstone's County Hall *coup*, has, on the face of it, and once you have forgotten about the firing squads in Whitehall, fairly modest aims.

'The top priority is lowering the public transport fares,' Livingstone said, before the House of Lords declared his cheap fares policy illegal. 'If we can get people cheaply about London it might become a really living town like Paris, and the demand for motorways would slacken. Then housing. Do you know what the Tories managed to build last year? Thirty-five houses – thirty-five, down from seven thousand! And we're going to have an enterprise board to open small factories . . . We must invest socially.'

'But can you put up rates without a limit?'

'We can now. Our rates come to about £500 million a year and a third of it from offices in Central London so that doesn't hurt our people. But the government wants to limit our power to raise money . . . It's getting more control over local authorities than Brezhnev has in Russia.

'Civil defence? We're not spending out on that. In the last war they evacuated London. Now they're going to use the army to keep people in. London's expendable, except for about 3,000 Very

Important People who they want to save. I don't think I've been invited to join them.'

And he added one of the ideas that does add considerably to the jollity of the young Labour councillors: 'We're going to spend the money they want us to use on things like the Dollis Hill bunker or making a new version of the banned BBC film *The War Game*.'

The man who has £500 million worth of rates a year to spend was born opposite the police station in Streatham where he could see the pigs ('The old-fashioned four-footed variety') they kept in the backyard. His parents met when his mother was a chorus girl and his father, on a noisy and bibulous leave from the Merchant Navy, created a disturbance in the theatre and then went behind the scenes to apologize.

'My father travelled all round the world,' said Livingstone. 'And you know what I admired about him? He was entirely without racialism. He and my mother were like all working-class Tories, they had to work very hard. They both had two jobs. My mother worked in a shop all day and was a cinema usherette in the evenings. My father was a window-cleaner who became a scene-shifter at night at the Streatham Empire. I never had to contend with religion. They worked so hard I spent most of my time with my grandmother.'

The 11-plus, that examination which has so often turned a blind eye to talent, failed Livingstone and he ended up at Tulse Hill Comprehensive School. There, in the year of Suez and Hungary, an imaginative teacher, Philip Hobsbawn, discussed politics with his class and pointed Ken's nose in the direction which would lead twenty years later to a life of almost monastic dedication to the austere god of local government, his cell being a Maida Vale bed-sit where he has a tank of salamanders for company.

'I sort of dropped out of school and I became a technician in a cancer research hospital. I had to give injections and look after the animals. I was about one step above a hospital porter. My interest was natural history and at that time I could have been deeply into the preservation of whales.'

Then he did teacher training at a college in South London – 'a terrible place, full of vicars' daughters from the Home Counties'. But before he could take up the work he was elected to Lambeth Council and in a year was vice-chairman of the housing committee. He became that rare thing, a totally professional local councillor. The whales, from then on, would have to look after themselves.

'What do you live on?' I asked.

'My pay and allowances from the council. Now it's £2,500 and £1,000 expenses.'

'Less than your secretary earns?'

'Oh yes. We're the lowest-paid people in the building.'

He shares a house, a lavatory and a kitchen with a group of medical students, goes to work on the Underground and used to read science fiction, although now he's too tired in the evenings to read anything.

'And the salamanders?'

'Interesting little things. I found them in France when they were tadpoles. The male produces a package of sperm and just leaves it around for the female to pick up and fit into herself.'

'That doesn't sound much fun.'

'I'll tell you one thing about salamanders. They're so awful to eat that nothing harms them.'

We sat in the tea room at County Hall among the plastic table-tops. Livingstone was wearing a dark brown safari jacket and a tie. He's a good-looking young man with a small moustache who smiles a great deal, talks ceaselessly and seems – and why not? – extremely contented. At times younger men in jeans and open-necked shirts came in with letters and he read them quickly. A twenty-four-year-old girl came in with a pile of notes and documents. She was Valerie Wise, daughter of the former Labour MP, Audrey Wise. 'She's in charge of our enterprise board,' Livingstone said. 'Chairperson's an awful word. Call her the Chair.

'When Harold Wilson was elected,' he went on, 'I was literally trembling with excitement. I thought, now poverty will be abolished. We drifted to the left as Harold Wilson failed to deliver. Then the Tories smashed us in the GLC election. We were left with only twenty-eight Labour members, but that was our chance.

We knew we'd have new members elected some time and we'd make sure that they'd be from the left. We got the party to set up a regional executive, we drafted a 70,000-word manifesto and introduced the reselection of members each four years. The result was that out of twenty-five new seats, two thirds went to the left-wingers and we got the average age of a councillor down from sixty-five to thirty.'

So Ken Livingstone's GLC revolution was quietly produced with the aid of a right-wing Labour government and a Tory victory.

The Chair had come back to join us with an iced orangeade and a cream bun. Did Livingstone think he might face a new challenge from the Left himself one day, I asked?

'He won't,' the Chair said, 'if he doesn't do the wrong thing.' And she smiled in a way that a lesser man than Ken might have found chilling.

'Has he done the wrong thing?'

'I think so. When he didn't offer an 11 per cent rise to the Underground workers.'

'We told London Transport they weren't bound by the government's 6 per cent limit on pay increases and we'd underwrite their rise,' said Livingstone. 'Sid Weighell of the Railwaymen's Union accused me of promising railway workers more; but that was just a move in the right–left struggle in the Labour Party. He wants to discredit Tony Benn.'

'You made a mistake there,' the Chair said.

'Valerie's my conscience of the Left,' Ken said. 'When I went out to look for new candidates I picked on young people like Valerie.'

'You put me here,' the Chair said, 'so you can't complain about me. That's what I always tell you.'

Livingstone used to turn up to the housing committee in jeans. After the Labour leader, Andrew MacIntosh, won the GLC elections, there was an election for a new leader of the Labour Party. Livingstone appeared that morning wearing a blue suit and a tie; it seemed that he knew he had won. MacIntosh, a Labour 'moderate', was deprived of the fruits of victory.

'Your marriage broke up,' I said. 'Was that because you work too hard?'

'I think that had a good deal to do with it.'

'Don't you regret not having children?'

'You can like children without having them yourself,' Mr Livingstone said. I supposed he was right, although the remark had a touch of the salamander in it.

'But you lead this extraordinarily austere life without any of the pleasures of a family.'

'I don't think you have to live like that to do what Ken does,' the Chair said.

'There you go, Valerie.' Mr Livingstone looked at the twenty-four-year-old head of the enterprise board with a sort of pity. 'Trying to hang on to the remnants of your private life.'

'What interests you apart from politics?' I asked the Leader. 'For instance, do you like music?'

'Oh, I play it all, from Tchaikovsky to Spirit. Particularly before I've got to make a political speech. It gets the adrenalin going.'

'But the Royal Opera House . . .'

The name of Covent Garden affects the New Left at the GLC like a mention of fox hunting, and I'd been warned that the new view of the arts was more likely to prefer steel bands in Woolwich to Donizetti in Bow Street. But Mr Livingstone didn't stop smiling.

'Horace Cutler, the Tory GLC leader, went along to lunch at Covent Garden and they took him for a million pounds. It was the most expensive lunch ever. We're not against centres of excellence,' Mr Livingstone sounded reasonable, 'but any extra money should go to local organizations, like the Battersea Arts Centre.'

'I'm not sure about the Battersea Arts Centre. Not while so many of my constituents need jobs,' said the Chair.

'But the National Theatre and Covent Garden must bring thousands of tourists to London,' I said.

'Tourists! I'm not rabid for tourism. Where I live, around Queensway, people have their shops taken over as boutiques and the restaurants stay open late at night and there are a lot of drunks. It's not much fun for people who live round the Finchley Road having tourists milling about at all hours, trying to pick each other up.'

'As a man of the New Left,' I asked, 'are you disappointed by the Social Democrat gains?'

'Not really, I can see the Tories vanishing and the Social Democrats becoming the right wing, which would be a small step in the right, or rather the left, direction. Then, of course, they'll collapse just as they did when they were in power as the right wing of the Labour Party.'

'So you are still cheerful?'

'Oh yes I am.' Livingstone never sounded less than perfectly contented.

'And the salamanders are still happy?'

At which Mr Livingstone sounded unusually serious. 'Salamanders have very primitive political reactions.'

A surviving handful of moderate Labour members have managed to frustrate Livingstone's attempt to lower the cost of school meals. 'There will be a few "moderates" in a Benn government who will manage to do the same thing,' he commented, everlastingly cheerful, 'You have to be prepared for setbacks.'

The New Left in the GLC, like Bennery itself, seems a very English phenomenon, with roots that go back to the Levellers and Oliver Cromwell. They have no time for boutiques or grand opera or abandoned Swedes around the Finchley Road. The atmosphere in the tea room at County Hall had been one of suppressed excitement, with smiles and jokes, as when a crowd of dedicated young people get together to produce, with tireless enthusiasm, a television show, or a repertory production, or, indeed, a system of local government.

Now Ken Livingstone was left alone, for a long evening's work, in his office with its 'Democracy Wall' on which his hate mail ('Get out you nigger-loving scum') is pinned up beside his cuttings from *Private Eye* ('They call me "Leninspart" – They got me very well really') and his faded photocopy of an invitation to the Royal

Wedding. ('We spent about forty seconds on that and all said, "Oh dear – why should we bother?" ')

Finally he'd go home to the bed-sit, to his miniature billiard table and shared loo and the waiting salamanders which he'd feed with earwigs and slugs. Under the safari jacket and the perpetual smile and the strong South London accent is a rather likeable, astute politician who knows his reforms have to be popular to succeed.

Indeed, the English have an endless talent for absorbing their English revolutions. The future may bring us Tony Benn as the prime minister who fails to abolish poverty, and the memory of another finally moderate GLC leader whose safari jackets and salamanders have sunk into the oak-panelled history of County Hall like the ancient whiff of Herbert Morrison's pipe tobacco.

'Will you listen to this, Caesar?'

MELVIN BELLI

'I just heard we won a case; and got a million dollars' damages.' Melvin Belli, with a head like the crumbling bust of a Roman senator, is one of the world's last great flamboyant advocates. His bulky and distinguished appearance would have reminded me of pictures of the late Sir Edward Marshall-Hall, if Sir Edward had been given to wearing Savile Row suits open at the wrist to display their flame-coloured silk lining, a gold watch-chain stretched across his lapelled waistcoat and Texas boots.

'You do a lot of investigating into personal injury cases?' Mr Belli asked, having discovered that I was also a lawyer, as I joined him and his family for dinner at the Savoy Grill.

'No investigating at all,' I told him. 'You see, we have things called solicitors . . .'

'Listen to that, Caesar!' Mr Belli said wonderingly to his law-student son. 'No investigating! Hey, when we heard a man upstate had lost his genitalia in an accident I had my investigators up there in an hour, and my partner was holding his wife's hand to get her used to trial lawyers. Then we make films like *A Day in the Life of a Boy in an Iron Lung* which won us the case against Cutter Chemicals, or we use huge blow-ups the size of that wall to show industrial burns. How do you fix your professional charges in a case?'

'Well,' I said vaguely, 'we have this thing called a clerk.' My mind was still, as a matter of fact, boggling at the thought of *A Day in the Life of a Man Who Lost His Genitalia*.

'Hey, listen to this, Caesar.' Mr Belli sank his distinguished head in the menu and his buttoned-down son looked puzzled but eager. 'I guess this clerk of yours must know a lot of law?'

'Not much, as a matter of fact, clerks don't, but they have a few drinks with solicitors in the pubs around the Temple and . . .'

'What share of the damages do you get?'

'Well. None at all really. You see . . .'

'I get a third,' said Mr Belli, ordering a bottle of burgundy with the air of a man who had just achieved a third of a million dollars. 'My firm will finance a case, pay the expert witnesses and make the movies. If we win we get a third of the take, if we lose it's a tax write-off. You got many partners in your law firm?'

'Well. Just me. You see, we aren't actually allowed partners.'

'No partners! I got a number of partners in the Belli Building, San Francisco. How did you come to qualify?'

'Well, it was largely a matter of eating dinners.'

'Eating dinners!' Mr Belli, clearly incredulous, turned his attention to ordering a portion of chopped onion to go with his smoked salmon. 'Hey, Caesar. Will you listen to this?'

'I want to see the sights of London,' said the fifth Mrs Belli, one-time Lia Triff, a sinuously beautiful lady of Graeco-Romanian origins in her late twenties, wearing a small, purple trilby hat at a rakish angle. 'I want to see your Hilton Hotel. I worked there one vacation as a student.'

At the end of the table, Melia Belli, six years old, her name a compound of those of her parents ('She's the real lawyer of the family,' Mr Belli said) tended to ignore me. No doubt she hadn't believed the story about dinners either.

From his ornate offices in the Belli Building ('You wait for your appointment in an area set in the Gay Nineties style. Colourful receptionists graciously serve coffee,' runs the publicity handout), Mr Belli easily makes the large income which he needs to finance his lawyer's way of life. Now he often cracks the sound barrier of million-dollar damages. In one case a furniture remover got $1,300,000 for a broken finger, which even Mr Belli admits was 'high'. A shield emblazoned in his office rightly proclaims him 'King of Torts'.

It wasn't always so, although Mr Belli, coming from a family of Swiss-Italian origins with a banker father, can never have been entirely poor. When he started he worked with the Catholic priest in San Quentin jail, who steered the hopeless appeals in capital cases his way.

He has an angry memory of going to see two of his clients hanged (the priest said they wanted him there as he was their only friend), and he walked through a room where the ropes were being stretched and the coffins waited. As the execution took place, a scratchy gramophone record played 'Clair de Lune', as the victims' last request.

The young trial lawyer saw the trapdoor drop and his clients' hands go white in death, 'like the picture of the Descent from the Cross'. He went home to share a bottle of Vat 69 with the priest and to curse the brutality of the law. 'That was the time I could have become a Communist,' he says.

Like all good and caring defenders, Mr Belli is against the death penalty, and has spoken out against the pathetic acceptance by the prison system of its complete failure to reform. He took on the defence of Jack Ruby because the prejudice against him was so strong in Dallas, and perhaps because Ruby's shooting of Lee Harvey Oswald was the first murder that all potential jurors had been able to watch on TV. No doubt it was to bring a little much-needed publicity to the defence that Mr Belli visited his client in jail wearing cowboy boots, a greatcoat with a Persian-lamb collar and sunglasses although it was a cloudy day.

However, he presented a careful and well-argued defence of insanity before a Dallas judge called 'Necessity' Brown (because, as they said, 'Necessity knows no law') who told him, at one point in the argument, to stop quoting 'nigger cases'. After the inevitable result, Mr Belli left Texas saying: 'I'm going to damn Dallas with every breath. There wasn't a law book cracked in the whole trial.' Of course, like Marshall-Hall, he got into trouble for unprofessional conduct, but the outburst was just and courageous.

'I guess you challenge a lot of jurors. You spend a couple of weeks maybe on the *voire dire*?'

'Well, hardly any at all. We've got three peremptory challenges, but they're not often used, you see . . .'

'Listen to that, Caesar. In San Francisco we get a book published every week, a directory of everyone on the jury panel. It tells you about their politics, if they went on any demonstrations, if they convicted last time. This publication costs $30 and you have to pay an extra $150 if you win the case.

'I figure if I like a juryman, he's going to like me. I don't like old ladies in criminal cases, they can be like *Arsenic and Old Lace*, killers under the embroidery. Italians, artists and writers are generous with damages; farmers and Scandinavians are mean. Doctors and nurses are mean also. Black juries in Detroit are generous in personal injury cases, but terribly tough in criminal cases. I like juries and I respect them. Our judges? Like everywhere, I guess. Ninety per cent of them are perfectly all right, and 10 per cent are drunks and bastards.'

The Belli family was on its way to Cortina in northern Italy. One year Mr Belli drove through his ancestral village in his brightly coloured Rolls the doors were all slammed, the inhabitants suspecting the arrival of a high-up Mafiosa.

Melvin Belli is a most upright lawyer, but I wonder if the system of sharing the winnings may not tempt some lesser men to fabricate evidence – even though the practice of taking cases on spec does enable the private American citizen to sue great corporations.

Mr Belli and I, as lawyers in San Francisco and London, lived very different lives, although, after years in courtrooms, we had many of the same instincts about judges, juries and the blunt over-simplication of the law. There was a rare silence as Mr Belli finished his wine. Then he said: 'I want to arrange an international seminar on personal injury cases. You should come over.' Caesar, Lia, even the child were looking at me. Clearly, they all thought I had a lot to learn.

'Remember compassion!'

R. A. BUTLER

Conservatives, like much else in our daily lives, seem to me to have grown less attractive with the years. The old variety could be imagined tramping England's misty acres, wearing gaiters and concerned in a genuine if patriarchal way with the sufferings of the poor.

The new Conservative appears all too often as a humourless suburban bank manager constantly assuring us that there's no more cake to go round, and regarding with disinterest or even contempt those dole queues which filled the young Harold Macmillan with such bitterness and rage.

So, in search of the old, humane heart of the Conservative Party, I rang the bell of a cavernous Whitehall flat and Lord Butler, a year or two before his death, came out of the shadows, stooping a little and smiling apologetically.

'You'd like a little whisky?' he said. 'My wife's not here and she said I mustn't make tea. I've never really got the hang of boiling a kettle.'

The place had a makeshift appearance, like the London flats of people whose homes and hearts are in the country. Most of the pictures were stacked against the walls, some Augustus Johns; a Vlaminck of a Flanders landscape which reminded its owner of Saffron Walden; a superb Degas drawing hung in the hall. Lord Butler, having held almost every great office of state and now retired as Master of Trinity, had been in New York lecturing on art.

'I had to make it clear what a lot of nonsense has been talked on the subject. I'm afraid Tolstoy got it in the neck for saying he didn't like Beethoven's Ninth but preferred the chanting of peasants. Plato got it wrong as well. He was against emotion. You must have emotion in art.'

'And in politics?'

'Certainly. A politician's nothing if he doesn't have emotion. You know who the best speaker I ever heard in the Commons was, and he spoke out of pure emotion?'

'Winston Churchill?'

'Not really. Winston prepared it all so carefully, all that rounded prose he dictated in bed between sips of champagne. Of course, he was a great old ramrod up us in the war; but the best speaker I ever heard was Aneurin Bevan.'

I remembered the speech in which Bevan had called the Tories vermin, and thought the tribute generous.

'When I started off in politics fifty years ago the agricultural wage in my constituency was twenty-nine shillings [£1.45] a week, which seemed wrong to me,' Lord Butler remembered. 'Then I toured the country and saw the pinched faces in the Labour Exchanges. So I spent a lot of time in the war on the committee to reconstruct health insurance and we gave all the help we could with the Beveridge Report.'

'Do you think the new Conservatives are less concerned?'

'Well, I'm sure they're honest, aren't they? But they're rather stern.' Lord Butler giggled and then straightened his face resolutely. 'Not all of them. Young James Prior – well, he's got a fine head of white hair now, and he made a speech the other day saying we've got to get on with the unions. I think he's come on rather well.'

'Did Churchill get on with the unions?'

'Oh yes. He rang me up at 2.30 one morning and said, "I thought you'd like to know we've settled with the miners." "Oh, really, Prime Minister," I said. "On what terms?" "On theirs, of course," he said. "Dammit, you've got to have electric light."

'I'm not sure Winston was really a Conservative. The party

offered itself to him and he made the sort of speeches they liked to hear about the Empire, but I'm not sure his heart was in being a Conservative.'

Lord Butler's eyes were shining. Somewhere deep inside he seemed to be suppressing another giggle. 'Winston used to ring me up before a Budget and say, "Remember compassion!" '

The ex-Master of Trinity was present at most of the crises of our modern history; and I asked him about Munich.

'Chamberlain knew almost nothing about foreign affairs and he couldn't get on with Eden. Well, Anthony behaved in an aristocratic sort of way and Chamberlain was a very good Mayor of Birmingham. He'd had a dreadful youth, his father thought young Neville was a failure and sent him out to an absolutely bloody sisal plantation in the West Indies. Personally, I thought Chamberlain had enormous courage.'

'In dealing with Hitler?' I asked, puzzled.

'No. In flying for the first time in his life in that little aeroplane at the age of seventy.' I had the distinct impression that Lord Butler was giggling again.

'Did you go in the aeroplane to Munich?'

'Oh, no. Alec Home went. I stayed at home. Chamberlain should never have said, "Peace in our time." It's a great mistake saying things like that.'

Inevitably I asked him about Suez. Had he seen the latest television play on the subject? 'Oh, yes. I think Anthony was very lucky to be acted so nicely. He had this liver complaint, you know. It was like waking up every morning with a terrible hangover. He was always a gent to the rest of the Cabinet, but he was frightfully peevish with his subordinates.

'He was never as determined or strong-minded as that actor suggested. Anthony was influenced by the first thing anyone said. And, of course, the negotiations with Israel went on so much longer than they did in the play. Anthony was terribly secretive about the whole thing. The first Humphrey Trevelyan, our ambassador in Egypt, knew about the crisis was when he was woken up by an awful thump in his back garden. We were bombing Cairo Airport.'

'Why was Eden so secretive?'

'Do you know, he was terrified of being stopped.'

'Who by?'

'Oh, everyone. The Americans and the UN and the service chiefs. Poor old Gladwyn was our ambassador in Paris and Anthony stayed with him when he was negotiating with the French; but he never told him a thing.

'What the TV didn't make clear is that I was acting prime minister when Anthony retired ill to Goldeneye, Ian Fleming's house in Jamaica. I got the International Monetary Fund money going again with the help of my friend George Humphrey at the US Treasury, and I actually got the troops out. It's all in Selwyn Lloyd's very boring book, if you can bear to read it. Harold Macmillan kept quiet at the time, which suited him rather well.'

'Were you surprised when Macmillan became prime minister?'

There was a small smile, another suppressed giggle – 'Rab' Butler's way of dealing with an old disappointment, and talking about the one Great Office he missed.

'I must say I was a bit flabbergasted,' he said. 'Winston rang me up and said he hoped I understood, but he was backing the older man. Of course, Macmillan loved going and talking to the Americans, so I was left in charge a lot of the time. I think people knew that, and they know I'm a good politician.'

'Did you like Macmillan?'

'Well, as I say, he started off with this enormous feeling about the poor in the North-East. He felt so strongly about them that he refused the Conservative whip and Baldwin thought he was far out on the left. But I must say in time the Chatsworth side of Macmillan began to take over. Like him? I'd rather you said I admired him.'

'And Ted Heath?'

'I'm afraid he is rather isolated now. If I'd been looking after him I'd never have let him have that confrontation with the miners. Baldwin always said there were two institutions you couldn't possibly fight.'

'What are they?'

There was no doubt about it, Lord Butler was laughing now. 'The National Union of Mineworkers and the Pope.'

Before he died 'Rab' Butler was planning to make a number of speeches in the Lords from the point of view of a humane Conservative. He was also reading Plutarch and *The Decline and Fall of the Roman Empire*.

'I especially like Gibbon on the Christians,' he said as he showed me to the door. 'They really had nothing to offer except bishops and the after-life, but they pushed on and came through rather well.'

Microchip Man

ROBB WILMOT

It had been a bad time for the great twin pillars of nineteenth-century morality, free enterprise and the gospel of work. As Sir Freddie Laker, the country's most popular capitalist, dropped like Icarus from the sky, the railway lines fell silent, the sidings inert, passengers at London Airport had to collect their own baggage and 25 per cent of commuters spent a week at home. Why, it was impatiently asked, can we not be more like the Japanese: loyal to the company, dedicated to the computer, prepared to work all the hours that God created for the sake of an upswing in our country's economy?

To discover if we can compete with Tokyo in the way of industrial enthusiasm, I visited Robb Wilmot, who is thirty-seven years old, makes £150,000 a year, works seven days a week and runs ICL, the British computer company which was, before his reinvigorating arrival a year ago, near to disaster. He has done an unprecedented deal with Fujitsu in which the Japanese company has agreed to supply him with large computers and what is known in microchip language as the 'state of the art' – the latest moves in that enthralling game in which electronic devices are planning to take over our lives.

International Computers Ltd has a headquarters in Carlton Gardens, London, at the top of a house where General de Gaulle once directed the French resistance to German technological expansion. In the outer office my first surprise was a butler in striped trousers and a black jacket, an ex-steward from the Cunard Line, who served me a cup of tea on a silver salver. As I was wondering if the pleasures of pre-war country house living survive only in the offices of young computer tycoons, I was joined by Joy Boyce, ICL's sympathetic public relations lady, herself a devotee of the computer industry, who gave me a short list of technical terms used in the strange world into which I had strayed.

' "Engineer",' she said. 'Means to see your way through a problem. Robb will "engineer" public relations.

' "Software" means abstract computer ideas and "hardware" means computers.

' "VLSI",' she added, 'means, "Very Large Scale Integration".'

'MIPS' means Millions of Instructions Per Second; some highly intelligent microchips, it seems, can absorb up to twenty-five MIPS, which is what sets them apart from Ray Buckton and the ASLEF drivers.

Miss Boyce told me that the government depended greatly on ICL for its computers, so when the company was in obvious trouble, the Department of Industry suggested Robb Wilmot, a young man who was managing director of the UK division of Texas Instruments.

'Robb is a very simple man, really,' she said. 'A family man. If he has any time off he likes to be out of doors with his family. But he's got charisma. He couldn't really have lunch with you because he seems to find it hard to sit still long enough for a meal. We try to see he gets his sandwiches.'

Then a door opened and the charismatic Mr Wilmot emerged, accompanied by an anxious-looking man with sandy hair who was talking about 'hot starts for the software'. Wilmot looks younger than thirty-seven: he was wearing glasses and a neat blue suit which might have had, only a few years ago, a row of pens in the breast pocket. Give him a pair of gloves and a long woollen scarf and you could see his face coming out of any northern university, ready for a quick half-pint before a long night studying the New Technology. He would be a quiet member of the group, with only an occasional smile or a dry little joke, clearly itching to get back to the diagrams.

We went into a panelled office and sat in black leather chairs. It was 5.30 and Wilmot looked suddenly pale and quite exhausted.

The butler entered with more tea on the silver salver and Miss Boyce and I both opened our notebooks, got out our pens, and prepared to transcribe the thoughts of Chairman Robb.

'My father worked in radar with the Ministry of Whatever-it-was. I should know.' Wilmot's eyes closed and I thought for a moment that he was about to drop off to sleep. 'Anyway it was signal research. At Malvern. My mother worked for the Electricity Board. You might say we had electricity in the family. Electricity was the first thing that interested me. When I left school I had a year before going to university. I worked for an electrical firm in Manchester. I was in general railway signalling and I worked out an electric system for the "Blackpool Pleasure Beach Express".'

The memory of this seemed to cause Mr Wilmot some nostalgic pleasure. He looked considerably more alert. Later I discovered that he invented microchips for Moulinex coffee machines and Hornby trains.

'I went to Nottingham University at seventeen and a half to read physics. At school I'd swum and played chess.'

'Tell me about your parents,' I said. 'What were their politics?'

'Neutral.'

'And your politics?'

'Oh, I'm neutral too.'

'So would it make any difference to your enthusiasm for your work if you were doing it in China, say, or Russia?'

It seemed that it would.

'China's at least eight years behind us,' said Mr Wilmot, 'electronically.'

'Was your family religious? Did you go to church, for instance?'

'Up to a certain age, I went. Church wasn't a great thing.'

'Religion,' I wrote. 'Neutral.' I couldn't see what Miss Boyce was writing.

So what did Robb's parents, the no doubt loving and supporting radar expert and the lady from the Electricity Board, believe in?

'They believed in working hard. Education meant working hard, they believed. They both came from farming families and had been brought up with the work ethic.'

'But what did you think was the purpose of all this hard work?'

'I was an engineering manager at twenty-three,' said Wilmot, 'I worked enormous hours. I wanted to learn in two years what it would take other people four to find out. It was a question of accumulating understanding.'

'And when did you meet your wife?'

'I ought to know that.' He closed his eyes and there followed a long silence. Again I feared he might crash out. 'When I was twenty-five, I think.'

'Then you were into microchips?'

'Oh yes. It's an industry that's moving very fast technically, and from a marketing point of view. It's intensely competitive. All sorts of people in our industry work a seventy- or eighty-hour week. It's quite normal.' He gave one of his rare, boyish smiles. 'And they die early.'

'And why do you like microchips so much?' I mean, I could understand anyone quite liking microchips, but Wilmot's total dedication to these cunning little objects was apparent as he became fully wakeful and bright-eyed, and answered with uninhibited enthusiasm.

'They're improving ten times every four years. They go faster and they get more complex and use less energy. They also cost less. Cars and aeroplanes are a static product. It's because they keep getting better that microchips have all the fun characteristics. Also they can change society.'

'In what sort of way?'

'We don't really know. The fascination is trying to push the technology to its limits. Already you can speak into a microphone and the letter you dictate will come up written on someone's television screen. A door will unlock itself at the sound of your voice or a computer will recognize a draughtsman's speech pattern when he says "transistor" – and draw one for him. You can make diagrams with a computer on a screen which will change with the varying rates of income tax, say, and save you pages of printout.'

'You think that when people have all these things it'll make life better for them?'

'They can use them for good or evil purposes.'

'So their work will be easier?'

'Oh, yes.'

'So they'll have more time off. I mean, they'll have more leisure.'

Mr Wilmot frowned. Leisure didn't seem to be a commodity he thought of highly.

'In fact aggressive nations with a high computer technology have very little leisure,' he hastened to assure me. 'The Japanese still put in long hours.'

'You enjoy working?'

'Of course I do. The time flies by.'

'What else do you enjoy? For instance, do you read books which aren't about electronics?'

'No. Some people get pleasure from artistic things, I suppose. I get my pleasure from seeing what we can make computers do.'

'You're not only a technical electrician. Now you're managing director of a company employing 23,000 people. Isn't managing people quite different from managing machines?'

'The technical side is managing people, too. I spend a lot of time going round the labs trying to get the engineers to do what I want. Doesn't always work, though.'

'What's your idea of managing people?'

'I think it's our duty to exploit people who want to be exploited. We need to drag them out and give them tough projects. People underestimate what they can do, particularly the English. We need to make engineers go out and talk to customers, do things they're not used to doing. We want them to be more aggressive.'

' "Aggressive" is a word you use a lot. What does it mean to you?'

'It means getting more of the market. Selling more.'

'Because you want to make more money?'

'No. Because I want to win.'

'You get paid an enormous salary, £150,000 a year. And you've got a £300,000 house in Kingston provided with the job. What's the point of all that money? You can't have any time to spend it.'

'I go on holidays abroad . . . and I've still got a house in Bedford to keep up. I mean, I go to Tenerife and Jamaica.'

'But you don't need all *that*. What's the use of it?'

I got another smile from the managing director and a calculation made without the benefit of computers in a voice as English as any union leader's.

'I suppose,' he said, 'it's the rate for the job.'

'Do you think we should be more like the Japanese?'

'No, we should be more like ourselves. We've got a lot of good computer engineers in England.'

'Or like the Germans?'

'As a matter of fact, the Germans are slow in adjusting to continual change, which is what our business is.'

But sadly, the English may not be entirely converted to computers yet. On a week-end expedition, Mr Wilmot went shopping with his two sons. Young Robert Wilmot picked up the Moulinex coffee machine, with its electronic brain designed by his father. 'You know,' said the managing director of ICL, 'there's a chip in that.' To which the shop assistant, who had overheard, said politely: 'Then I'll change it immediately.'

It was half-past six. The butler was mixing me a Campari soda on the salver. Robb Wilmot had another two hours of meetings before he went home to his lattice-windowed, five-bedroomed Kingston house, to sit by the stone fireplace and watch a videotaped *Horizon* programme before collapsing into bed. The next day he was flying to South Africa, one of the many countries in which ICL has a subsidiary company.

'Don't you find doing business in South Africa distasteful?' I asked. 'I mean, what do you think of the politics there?'

'South African politics?' said Mr Wilmot. 'I'm neutral.'

Of course, I should have remembered.

The new manager of ICL is, no doubt, the sort of young 'aggressive' businessman we all think we want. Just as I suppose we want doors that fly open at His Master's Voice, machines which will do artwork on request and letters from the bank manager flashing, without an instant's delay, upon the television screen.

I went out into the London evening and thought of all those commuters who were no longer trying to get to work during a rail strike, but sitting at home, getting to know their wives, tinkering with their cars or watching the slow emergence of their crocuses. I thought, with some affection, of all those workers who somehow don't care for being stretched, and I thought of Robb Wilmot, who told me that the trick of management was getting 23,000 people all pointing in the same direction. His energy is prodigious. In fact he works as hard and frenetically as many comparatively lowly paid people in films, the theatre and television.

For him, the microchip would appear to be a sort of pure art form, and with it he can do without the enthusiasm of politics, the consolations of religion or the revelations of literature. Of course, he won't be able to stand the pace for ever. He plans to retire while he is still young and start a company of his own. No doubt he'll be selling computers.

Eric Bartholomew and the 'Wellma Boy'

ERIC MORECAMBE

Mrs Sadie Bartholomew, usherette at the Odeon, thought she only had to walk down the street in Morecambe in the 1930s with her boy Eric and he would be discovered by a big-shot producer and snatched off to Hollywood to join Fred Astaire and Bing Crosby and Abbott and Costello on the silver-starred cover of *Picturegoer*.

Although not translated to Hollywood, Eric is now in what could be thought of as the English equivalent: a big house next to a golf course, picture windows looking out on the Hertfordshire countryside, handsome oil paintings of hunting scenes and landscapes under snow, lace antimacassars on comfortable chairs, a funny, gentle and understanding wife, Joan, grown-up children and an adopted son.

It can't be far from the height of Sadie's ambition. Eric is not only England's most popular comedian, he must be near to being our most popular person.

'How are you?' I asked him, as Joan, the stage-struck ex-soubrette who'd met him when they were on the same bill at the Empire, Edinburgh, poured coffee.

'How am I? I really don't know. I don't dare look. See on that tree there . . . a bullfinch?'

Eric the ornithologist looks remarkably well, pink and relaxed. They took veins from his legs and put them in his heart, and now, to everyone's delight, he's back with his put-upon partner to treat our television screens as the best end of the pier show anyone ever dreamt of.

'My father worked for the corporation,' the one-time Eric Bartholomew told me. 'That is, he was a labourer in Morecambe. A big, gentle man. He was a bit of a whistler, only with pursed lips. Not like Uncle Dick, who could stick his fingers in his mouth and whistle professionally. Mother was the ambitious one. She got me a plank to tap-dance on and made me a cut-down Fred Astaire set, top hat, white tie and tails, and put me in for "Go As You Please" concerts.

'Then mother was working on the Centre Pier where the concert party performed "if weather inclement". Three of the girl dancers were having a benefit and they asked mother if I could go on with them, so I blacked up as G. H. Elliott, the chocolate-coloured coon, or was it T. S. Eliot? I can't remember, it's so long ago.

'Then I did an audition for Jack Hylton at Hoylake and within months I had my first professional engagement with Bryan Michie's "Discoveries" at the Empire, Nottingham. What did I do? Sang "I'm Not All There" and imitated Flanagan and Allen. I was thirteen at the time.'

So Sadie and Eric Bartholomew set out on the road and the young discovery was making £5 a week while Dad, the not-quite-professional whistler, stayed at home and worked for the council for thirty-eight shillings (£1.90) a week. And then came the event which may rank with Gilbert bumping into Sullivan, or the Lunts' first date.

'Ernie was a "Discovery" too, but I didn't really know him. Then one night we were playing the New Theatre, Oxford, and there was a knock at the door of the digs, and it was young Ernie Wiseman with nowhere to sleep. So mother went on to the couch and she put Ernie and me to bed together, which was allowed in those days.'

So began the great duet which is really the comedy of an English marriage, missing out the sex as many English marriages do. Not only are Eric and Ernie frequently in bed together in their television shows, their quarrels are all domestic, the wild ambitions of the pushy little husband being forever wrecked and frustrated by the anarchic housewife in the apron and the specs.

Eric and Ernie first appeared together as a double act at the Empire, Liverpool, when Eric was fourteen. 'We stole gags from other comics. Mother said we did a lot of blue jokes, but we didn't understand them. We sang "Run Rabbit Run" and "Why Does My Heart Go Boom?" At one time Ernie was the comic and I was the "Wellma Boy".'

'You were the what?'

'The feed. The one who came on to the stage and said "Wellma boy, and what are you going to do tonight?" '

When Ernie came back from the Merchant Navy and Eric from his time as a Bevin Boy (down the mines where his heart trouble began) they reversed roles, as married couples will from time to time, and Mr Wise became the 'Wellma Boy'.

They did fourth spot and the second after the interval round the Moss Empires for £27 10s. (£27.50) a week. They played the broker's men with lines like 'All the little elves are playing with themselves' and 'Nine months gone, and no sign of Robin' in endless Christmas pantomimes.

They learned from Jimmy James and Sydney Howard (a gentle comedian who walked with his hands spread out) that impeccable timing which is the basis of their technique. They admired George Formby's way with a song, 'Although as a comic,' Eric says, 'Formby was about as funny as a cry for help.'

'I was on a bill with Adelaide Hall and her American husband said the name Eric Bartholomew didn't look good on a marquee. I didn't know what he was talking about. I thought a marquee was a sort of tent. Anyway, he told me that Eddie Anderson, a black dancer, took his name from Rochester where he was born, so I became Eric Morecambe.

'When I had a heart attack in Leeds, it was like a Brian Rix farce. I was helpless in my Jensen in the deserted streets at about one o'clock in the morning, and the only living human being around was this man who'd been in the Territorial Army.

'I asked him if he could drive, and he drove my £7,000 motor-car like a tank for miles. Then he had to wake someone up at the hospital. Finally, as they wheeled me into intensive care, I saw him standing over me. He whispered in my ear: "Can I have your autograph before you go . . . ?" '

The man who is now and ever will be Eric Morecambe laughed inordinately at the memory. It's splendid to face disaster in stoic silence. To turn it into comedy requires courage of a high order.

The Elusive Social Democrat

ROY JENKINS

When I met Roy Jenkins he was in an understandably good mood. He had conceived the idea of a new party which was to 'break the mould of British politics', and no one was yet impertinent enough to ask if it were going to serve up the same old trifle. Nor had the Social Democratic Party been put to any kind of electoral test. It remained, after Mr Jenkins's initial lecture, a promised flight on an unscheduled aeroplane to . . . where exactly? Perhaps back to the halcyon days when he was Chancellor of the Exchequer and inflation was 5 per cent, there were a mere 500,000 unemployed, we had nothing worse than Mr Harold Wilson to irritate us, and you could take a girl out to dinner and get change for a ten-pound note, providing, of course, that you had a ten-pound note.

'You must be feeling happy about the public opinion polls,' I said. These wayward guides had just pronounced in favour of an SDP government, whatever that might turn out to be.

'I'm glad to feel there may be a break-up of the old, ossified structure of British politics, and that things could change for the better. I'm also enormously relieved,' Mr Jenkins smiled. 'About eight months after my lecture I felt more isolated than I ever have in my life. I thought I'd condemned myself to loneliness and a hopeless enterprise.'

'Will you be the leader of the new party?'

'I'm not thinking about that. I'm not really thinking about this in career terms. Shirley's enormously popular . . .'

'But you'll be back in Parliament?'

He gave a small sigh – 'I suppose I'll have to, that depends on the electorate' – and a discreet giggle – 'I do assure you, my most obsessive desire is not to get back into Parliament.'

'A criticism of you is that you've always had things too easy. And now you want to come back from a highly lucrative job in Europe and find a new party waiting to welcome you instead of fighting things out in your old one. Denis Healey said you want everything handed to you on a plate.'

'Master Healey! Master Healey!' Jenkins was clearly delighted with this form of address for his former colleague.

'Well, he seems to be fighting inside the Labour Party,' I said.

'Is he? The old tank! He's left it a bit late. His resilience sometimes spills over into complacency.'

'But do you want to get things without really fighting for them?' I remembered the unkind words of a bright young Labour MP: 'The only thing that Roy Jenkins ever fought for was a table for two at the Mirabelle.'

'The Palm without the Dust,' Mr Jenkins was triumphant. 'You see, I'll give you a better phrase. That's out of my book on Charles Dilke. No. I don't think I want the Palm without the Dust. It wasn't easy being chancellor in 1967 to 1970. I spent a long time fighting my European corner. If I'd been able to go along with the Wilson zig-zag on Europe I could have stayed deputy leader and I might have become leader of the Labour Party.'

It is possible to say that success has come easily to Roy Jenkins. He was a Welsh grammar-school boy who got a first at Balliol. In the Royal Artillery he saw some stirring action on Salisbury Plain, where one of the guns scored a direct hit on the general's car. Left-wing stalwarts should note that Captain Jenkins's gun was clearly exonerated. He became an MP in 1948 and from early minor government posts rose steadily to become Home Secretary and Chancellor of the Exchequer.

The encounter with him was, as always, extremely pleasant. He's sixty-one, red-faced, taller than you'd imagine, inhabiting a cavernous flat in a big Victorian house in Kensington Park Gardens, at the desirable end of Portobello Road. He has, like Norman St

John Stevas, the admirable quality of looking as if he found politics a bit of a joke, and also shares the lamented ex-Leader of the House's habit of saying 'orften' and 'lorst'. He calls his sitting room 'agreeable'; it is very large with a lot of desks, sofas, vaguely contemporary paintings and books. He also has a house near Wantage. As we talked he drank whisky and smoked a cigar in the old Harold Wilson style.

'My father was a remarkable man. I've been thinking about him. He'd have been a hundred years old this year.'

'And *his* father?'

'My grandfather was a Welsh miner. He used to give me a gold sovereign every year.'

'A rich miner?'

'A generous miner.'

Arthur Jenkins, the born-again Social Democrat's father, also started work in a Monmouthshire pit. But he went on to Ruskin College, Oxford, and, strangely enough, to Paris for two years where he learnt to speak French better than Roy could when he went to the European Commission. In Paris, Jenkins *père* became the admirer of the old French Socialists, Jean Jaurès and Marx's grandson Jean Longuet. He came back to England to become an official in the Mineworkers' Union, a member of the national executive of the Labour Party and, from 1935, a Labour MP.

'Your father was a Methodist. Did God play a large part in his life?'

'I think it was mainly that he enjoyed playing and singing Welsh hymns in a loud voice.'

'What would he have thought of your leaving the Labour Party?'

There was a pause. 'Perhaps I find it distasteful to disinter his bones to answer those sort of questions. But I certainly wouldn't be ashamed to explain what I'm doing to him.'

'All right, then. Who did you admire? When you went into Parliament?'

'Attlee I knew well. I admired Ernie Bevin and Stafford Cripps. From a distance, of course. You always admired Stafford Cripps from a distance. I admired Hugh Gaitskell immensely.'

'Yet Gaitskell stayed in the party to fight and fight again, when he lost to the left wing.'

'You forget. He held most of the levers of power. He had the Parliamentary Party by two to one, the national executive, and a sizeable number of the trades unions on his side. And he actually said that if he'd lost twice on nuclear disarmament he'd have gone. He'd have left the party.'

'So would Hugh Gaitskell be a Social Democrat now?'

'Of course, but once again, I don't think we should disinter the bones of the saints.'

'I've heard there was far more bitterness inside the Labour Party at the time when Gaitskell was fighting the Clause 4 resolution [the reaffirmation of Labour's commitment to nationalize the means of production, distribution and exchange] than in its present controversies. There was all that tension and yet the Labour Party didn't split in those days?'

'Some tension's good for a marriage. Unless it becomes a desire to destroy the other partner.'

'But for years and years the left wing of the party have been defeated, been in a minority. But they didn't split off. Why can't the right wing accept a period of being in a minority in the Labour Party?'

Mr Jenkins, puffing at his cigar, had a think about that. 'When the Left were in a minority it was only being asked to postpone the promised day, perhaps to wait longer to nationalize another industry. It was a negative thing for them. But we are now being asked to positively defend policies, like the trade unions' election of a leader or unilateral disarmament, or Common Market withdrawal, with which we could not possibly agree.'

'But doesn't politics depend on power? The Conservatives have got the power of big business and the City. The Labour Party have the power of the unions. What's your power base, apart from vaguely good intentions?'

'I think that's a wild simplification,' Roy Jenkins replied with some force. 'After all, a large number of trade unionists voted Conservative. I think there is a complex intermediate group, and

I don't think people vote entirely from material interests. There's room for a bit of idealism too.'

'Do you think you'll ever convert the old entrenched right-wing working-class Labour member, like Roy Mason, for instance?'

A silence fell behind the cigar smoke. Roy Mason might, Mr Jenkins conceded, prove a hard nut to crack. As he poured another drink and waited with great courtesy for the next question, I felt that I was getting only fleeting glimpses, through the lush vegetation, of that charming and retiring animal, the Social Democratic Party. What, for instance, was Socialist about it?

'Oh, Socialism!' The thought seemed to cause Jenkins much quiet amusement. 'I haven't used that word for years. If you mean nationalizing the means of production, distribution and exchange . . . That leads to disaster. I mean, just look at Poland!'

There was a silence. Not even the bones of Jean Jaurès and Karl Marx's grandson were heard to rattle.

'Then if there isn't going to be any Socialism, why not join the Liberal Party?'

'We believe we can tap more support by a friendly relationship with them. We have no real differences with the Liberals – at least in the short term. We believe in government intervention, and not *laissez-faire*, market-place economics. The state must create employment, and lean against the unfairness of market forces.'

'All right. No Socialism. Some state intervention. What does the Council for Social Democracy really believe in?'

'In a sentence, I believe in introducing humanitarian conscience and reform; concern for those who don't easily survive in a rough world.'

I wrote it down carefully and looked at it. It seemed like the parson's pronouncement on sin – he was against it. It was a creed that might be repeated by almost anyone from Lord Hailsham to Tony Benn. All the same, concern for those who don't survive easily hasn't been a glowing characteristic of the 1980s. The rare Social Democratic animal had made another brief but charming appearance between the trees and I attempted to pursue it through the undergrowth.

'You were in power in a right-wing Labour government for many years. Is what we're being offered a return to right-wing Labour rule? I'm not saying that would necessarily be a bad thing, but why would it be any better now?'

'We had leadership compromising with the Left.'

'What were the compromises?'

'Too much inflation in the 1974 government, and trades union legislation that gave the unions too much of what they wanted on a plate. And we had instability in political direction, which eventually led to left-wing control.'

When he is in the country, Roy Jenkins listens to opera records – mostly Verdi, Mozart and Strauss – and is one of those who can read the work of Anthony Powell. 'I'm mentioned in Evelyn Waugh's diary,' he told me, 'Waugh says: "A friend asked me to dine with people she thought I'd like to meet. How mistaken she was." ' Well, Mr and Mrs Jenkins didn't take to Mr Waugh either.

I asked him about the Obscene Publications Act which he promoted, and clearly hadn't anticipated how much legal confusion had flown from its mysterious definitions.

'I'm not too worried about that situation. I really think that, if pornography were the only evil in society, we'd be extremely lucky.' This is where Roy Jenkins is at his best, when he is looking back, unashamed, on some of the advances in personal freedom obtained in the 1960s.

'We had our liberal hour, when we passed the Sexual Offences Act which stopped all homosexuals being criminals. I'm not ashamed of that. We mustn't slip back into illiberal attitudes. You see, there are two strands in the Labour Party.' And here, the Social Democratic animal appeared in a shaft of sunlight and looked singularly attractive. 'The libertarian strand and the authoritarian puritan strand. By and large, the libertarians have come with us and the others have stayed behind.'

'What do you think of all those jokes about you and claret?' I had to ask.

'Mildly irritating. I suppose it's like Churchill's cigar or

Baldwin's pipe.' Mr Jenkins seemed to be assuming prime ministerial status, but with becoming modesty. 'I mostly drink rather cheap wine and I like very simple food.' And then he added as though it were a surprise to him, and would be to me also, 'I like shepherd's pie and fish-cakes.'

The question is, I suppose, whether Mr Jenkins will be able to bridge that great gulf which lies between claret and fish-cakes (the frozen, Tesco variety), or will he fall, like many a well-meaning politician before him, into the great chasm that divides these delicacies and be lost to us for ever?

A Little Bit of Charisma

MICK JAGGER

The quest for Mick Jagger seemed, for a long while, to be destined to frustration. The middle-aged Puck, with his retinue of some 150 followers and his fellow Stones, came and went and proved a hard act to follow. The Dionysus of Dartford intoxicated his devotees by the stadiumful and then, as rare things will, he vanished. The Rolling Stones' London office was friendly, but short on hard news. 'You want to see Mick?' said the girl on the telephone. 'Terrific! Well, I think he's asleep. Well, somewhere out of London. Well, we think he could meet you at four o'clock but we're not sure where exactly.'

Later she telephoned and said, 'Mick says couldn't you meet him in Frankfurt tomorrow?'

'No,' I said, 'not really.'

'Oh,' she said. 'Terrific!'

Some days later she telephoned and suggested I talk to Mick at the Three Kings Hotel in Madrid at two o'clock on the next Thursday afternoon. After extensive work on the Madrid telephone directory had failed to discover the existence of any such hotel, we phoned the Stones' office with this disconcerting news.

'Oh, really?' said the girl on the phone. 'Terrific!'

So, at four o'clock on the Thursday afternoon, I came reeling in from a temperature of 97 degrees in the streets of Madrid to the comparatively cool recesses of the Palace Hotel. Spain had changed from the days when I remembered it, the grim end of the Franco régime. Now pop music was blaring from the news-stands which displayed *Playboy* and *Penthouse*, the artists in the public gardens were painting numberless portraits of J. R. Ewing and Princess Di, and on a football ground the night before an audience finally liberated into the democratic way of life had been watching the tireless Mr Jagger bounding, stripped to the waist and in gold lamé Turkish trousers, when they were hit by a sudden thunderstorm and a number of huge, gaily coloured balloons fell upon their heads.

'I bet you never thought I'd be here,' said Mr Alun Edwards, the Stones' public relations man who had appeared, wearing grey woollen shorts and a sweat shirt, by the porter's desk. He looked, as he approached me through the shadows, to be about eighteen years old.

'Can you assure me I'm going to meet Mr Jagger?' I asked him.

'I tell you,' he smiled winningly. 'Nothing's certain in this world. There could be a fire or a riot, couldn't there? Barring that, I promise you, you will meet Mick.'

'Well,' I said, 'lead me to him.'

'Mick's just having breakfast at the moment. Look. Why don't you go up to your room, have a cup of tea, and I'll come and knock on your door.'

Not much more than an hour later Mr Edwards did exactly that. Mr Jagger, it seemed, was ready to receive me in audience. I got off the bed feeling rather as Sir Galahad might have done when he was told there was someone at the front door who had come to deliver the Holy Grail, and would he please come down and sign for it.

'You must have got on well with your father.'

Joe Jagger, a school PE instructor, who now works for the Council of Physical Recreation, allegedly brought up the young Mick to be the sort of athlete who covers the same distance as a football referee during his rock concerts. It was father Jagger, according to recent publicity, who gave his son that fanatic interest in cricket which is the hallmark of a Stone coming eventually to rest.

'No,' said Mick Jagger. 'I didn't get on with him, not really.'

'Why?'

'I suppose because I wanted to go out and play the guitar, and he wanted me to go to work. Usual thing.'

'Was he religious?'

'No. I think his generation had had religion so heavy that they turned against it. My mother was more. Our family was just into the middle class, I suppose; you know, "At least we don't work in a factory." I don't think Dad was very left wing. I think Mum voted Labour, but when I asked them about it they used to say, "Ssh. It's a secret ballot." And they'd never tell me.'

'No one in the family was a performer?'

'Oh, I had a couple of uncles who did music-hall songs, and stood on a soap box talking about religion and all that. I suppose in the Depression you did anything for money. Mother could sing the songs she heard on Radio Luxemburg. Dad was tone deaf.'

'You went to Dartford Grammar School?'

'I had a decent education. I was in the Arts Sixth, there was only about six of us in there. I used to like reading Rimbaud and Baudelaire and that other one . . . Maupassant. Let's say I was exploring the possibilities of decadence. I heard someone say that the most decadent poet ever was William Blake.'

'You like Blake?'

'Of course I do. Well, music was all my life, all I thought about. We were playing in pubs and clubs. I'd known Keith Richards at my junior school and he had parents who were more tolerant than mine. There was Alexis Korner.' (What was he referring to? I thought perhaps some difficult traffic intersection outside Birmingham. Later I discovered that Mr Korner was an artist and broadcaster and early patron of the Stones.) 'He's always doing voice-overs for fish fingers and things now, but he had this club in Ealing, and the first band that actually played American blues music. I used to sing there sometimes.'

'Then you got to the London School of Economics. Why economics?'

'I don't know. Everyone at school was doing science. I thought I should do something between art and science, so I chose that. I managed to master the basics, but we were in the top ten by that time. I was making about £500 a week. I went to the Registrar and he was very nice about it and said, well, if I didn't make it in music I could come back. Really we had it pretty easy. No hard struggle. I think that's good. People who have to struggle to get to the top go over the top when they get there. Of course, we had to have a gimmick.'

'What was yours, being the bad boys when the Beatles were good? I mean, being the ones the mums didn't like their daughters to listen to?'

'Yes. That was a publicity stunt really, for the Beatles *and* us. We were uncouth, that's what we were. We tried to get as far away as possible from what you were meant to be like in those days.'

'What was that?'

'Well, you know . . .' And Mr Jagger smiled as he said, with long-drawn-out contempt. 'Like Cliff Richard. You didn't smoke, you didn't screw anyone and you drank *milk*!'

At thirty-eight, Mick Jagger's face is rutted, deeply lined, like the face of a jockey or a sailor, someone who is forever up against a high wind. It is a face which no longer disturbs the mums as it glowers from the walls of half the world's teenage bedrooms: the face of a dreamy young eighteenth-century aristocrat with too much experience and a taste for poetry, and of that same aristocrat's worldly-wise, insolent and cynical lackey. He talks in a slow, Dartford drawl which turns most of what he says into a deliberate parody of itself. Often the end of his sentences is signalled by a sudden smile which is quite dazzling.

So we sat in the largest suite in the Palace Hotel, Madrid, in front of a huge, ill-tuned television set which showed the Italian game against Poland darkly, in stripes of colour like a faded football sweater. Mr Jagger was wearing a pair of wide khaki shorts, drinking a bottle of beer and occasionally interrupting his thoughts to watch an action replay. In the background a girl, dressed in a slightly crumpled, off-the-shoulder white lace dress as for the last act of *Carmen*, poured drinks and made phone calls. Alun Edwards was somewhere stage left.

'Mick will have dinner after the show either with Jerry Hall if she's in town or Prince Rupert, his financial adviser,' Mr Edwards told me. 'Then he'll go to bed around three. He's not like Keith. Keith'll stay up four nights without any sleep and then he'll crash out completely.'

'Go on,' I said to Mr Jagger. 'You were telling the story of your life.'

'Nineteen sixty-seven, it was. We got into trouble with the law. I was in jail twice, and that's not a very nice place to be, I tell you.'

He was arrested for possessing four amphetamine tablets, which he had bought quite legally in Italy. For this offence the judge at Chichester imposed a prison sentence and later made a speech to the Horsham Ploughing and Agricultural Society in which he quoted the *Julius Caesar* line about 'You blocks, you stones, you worse than senseless things', and said the law 'had cut the Stones down to size'.

'The papers were against us,' Mick Jagger remembered. 'All of the gutter press were on about public morality and dens of vice and that. They went on about it for weeks. I think that's why Brian Jones drowned himself in the end, although it was never proved exactly.'

'But *The Times* wasn't against you,' I said. To his eternal credit, Mr Rees-Mogg, the then editor, wrote an editorial entitled 'Who Breaks a Butterfly upon a Wheel?', protesting against the remarkably silly sentence. John Osborne wrote to *The Times*, Michael Havers pleaded the Jagger cause in court, and in the end the leading Stone slid out of Wandsworth into the bosom of the Establishment.

'It was really funny,' Mick Jagger smiled. 'The press put us inside and then the press got us out.'

'I suppose the argument was that you should set an example to young people in the way you lived. Did you ever feel that?'

'Not really. Anyway, young people wouldn't have known how we lived if it hadn't been for the newspapers. It was all a bit of a hang-up for us. I mean, after that I wasn't allowed into the States for about two years.'

'But apart from that, the sixties was a marvellous time for you.'

'People forget that. It was a good time really: 400,000 unemployed! Only 400,000 . . . That was all it was. In the days of "Jumping Jack Flash" and "Goodbye Ruby Tuesday".'

'And Harold Wilson,' I said.

'Well, yes. Swinging London. It must be horrible to start out and never find a job. It must be awful!'

'You're interested in politics?'

'Oh yes. I used to have those lunches, didn't I, with Tom Driberg in the Gay Hussar!'

The vision was enthralling. The gossip columnist and future Chairman of the Labour Party and Jumping Jack Flash discussing the rights and wrongs of nationalization over the cherry soup and goulash in a small Hungarian restaurant in Soho. But Mr Jagger went on before I had time to relish the situation.

'Politics is sort of interesting now. It's all so splintered. Even the SDP's splintered.'

'Do you think we've got less concerned about each other, politically nastier?'

Mr Jagger was engrossed in an action replay and I tried again. 'What do you think about the Falklands affair, for instance?'

'A most unnecessary war. And I hate the idea of people dying. English and Argentinian.'

'So what *are* your politics exactly?'

'In America it's easier for me to be political. There's a sort of dialogue between politicians and entertainers. They can't get huge hand-outs from millionaires any more, so they need concerts to finance their campaigns. So there's this sort of dialogue.'

'I mean, Cliff Richard is not political. So are you?'

'No. Cliff Richard isn't.' Another dazzling smile.

'So what would you say your political beliefs were?'

On the television set someone scored a goal. Mr Jagger gulped beer in silence.

'I mean, have you ever given a concert for a politician?'

'Let's say . . . it's been suggested.'

'Could we say you're not exactly right wing?' I prepared to make a note.

Once again Mr Jagger gave his attention to the World Cup. There was the sort of silence which meant, perhaps, that a world star was not about to alienate half his audience. I tried again.

'Well. Would you perform in aid of Mr Reagan?'

'Not Mr Reagan. Naaow!' The final word was a long-drawn-out murmur of incredulity and derision.

'Or for Mrs Thatcher?'

There was a longer silence. Nothing much was going on on the football field. Carmen looked at Mr Jagger with large, dark, respectful eyes.

'Let's say,' Mick Jagger said, with a certain amount of caution, 'she'd never ask.'

'The seventies was a bit of a down period,' Mr Jagger was saying. 'Everyone rips you off in this business and I'd been ripped off considerably. I really had *no money!* I went to live in the South of France. I got married. Things like that. I didn't do much work. It was the flower-power time, you were meant to be mystical. It was important in a way, but there's not much left of it now.'

'Are you at all religious?'

'Not *one* religion, if that's what you mean. I suppose I'd have a bit of Christian, bit of Muslim, bit of Buddhism. But not *just* one.'

'Do you believe in immortality?'

'What a question to throw me in the middle of the World Cup!'

'But do you?'

'Not of my personality. Not at all. That's going to stop completely . . . But I suppose a few songs might trickle on for . . .'

'Posterity?'

'Well, it's possible.'

'Do your songs have any sort of message for people?'

'Well, if you believe the Spanish papers . . .'

The concert the night before, once the rain had stopped, had been an undoubted triumph, and the notices, in a country starved of the Stones for so many years, ecstatic.

'It was the same in the Communist *and* the Catholic papers,' Alun Edwards said. 'They called it a magical, mystical experience. We've never had such heavy notices, not even from the *Guardian*.'

'No, I don't really try and tell them anything,' Mr Jagger said.

'Do you think you've changed young people at all, by your music?'

'Let's say perhaps . . . Just a ti—ny, ti—ny bit.'

'Liberated them?'

'Let's say, perhaps.'

'When was your most exciting moment?'

'The day I first bought a pink Cadillac in Los Angeles.'

'We've got some funny gigs in front of us,' said Mr Jagger.

'Turin,' said Alun Edwards. 'Let's face it, the Communists control the music scene in Italy and the Catholics may protest. Then we've got boat-loads of Moroccan fans coming to Naples. Imagine that, Africans coming to Europe to listen to rock music! It's completely unknown.'

At Newcastle the chief constable found the Stones fans far better behaved than football crowds, and the directors of the stadium, large men with cigars and camel-hair coats who read the *Daily Express*, Mr Edwards said, 'Brought their wives, who loved it.' At Wembley, the thirty to thirty-five age-group came feeling nostalgic. When they were in London, the Stones played in their old stamping ground, the '100 Club', without publicity to a small audience. Perhaps the group are nostalgic for their own past, just as we are.

'What do you read?' I asked Mick Jagger. 'There must be a lot of time, travelling. Do you read a lot?'

'Oh yes. I read. Biographies mostly.'

'Whose biography, for instance?'

'I'm reading about Rasputin now.' His smile was at its most innocent. 'Now there *was* a person with a bit of charisma.'

So the rolling continues. The two huge sets, the growing retinue and charter plane for the group, were ready to set out to meet the Communists in Turin and the African fans in Naples. The Rolling Stones, named after an old song by Muddy Waters, seem more than ever in these grim times part of our contented past, the old, permissive, swinging sixties. About two and a half million people have filled the stadiums on this tour, desperate to hear the music that once made us jump for joy or anger.

'They say you run fifteen miles during a performance,' I said to Mick Jagger. 'How long can you go on doing that?'

'Not *that* exactly. But I can go on giving some sort of show. I don't think you need ever stop. Not if you're an entertainer.'

Trial by Television

MIAMI LAWYERS

English lawyers have a saying, 'Justice must not only be done, but must be seen to be done.' The Supreme Court of Florida has improved on it: 'Justice must not only be done, but must be seen to be done, if necessary between commercials for dog food and pantyhose, in prime time on television.'

In England an artist with a sketch pad at a murder trial would be instantly ejected; we are not even allowed to stand in the street and photograph customers going into the Old Bailey. In the courts of Florida there is a new position, apart from the judge's bench, the lawyers' seats and the chair for the accused: it is marked 'Television Camera', and a judge has been known to rebuke defence advocates for getting between His Honour and the camera's all-seeing, all-publicizing eye.

What is television in court? A sign of democratic government in a free society; or the final sickness of a time when life has all but disappeared up the cathode-ray tube and murder, justice and execution have become, like brain surgery, childbirth and war, subjects for mass entertainment?

In an attempt to find some answer to those questions I journeyed to Dade County to visit the Miami legal profession. I am an English lawyer, as strange to the ways of American courtrooms as the Miccosukees and the Seminoles, those Indian tribes who once enjoyed undisputed domination over Miami Beach.

Florida is a state in the Deep South of America. Traditionally right-wing Democrat, it is the home of oranges, Cuban refugees and those other refugees from a long, hard life of money-making in the cold north, the very old. It is a great place for facelifts, open-heart surgery and wearing your jewellery on the beach, for, after all, you may not have very long to wear it anywhere. Signs say, 'Get your blood pressure taken here!' There are luxurious hotels along the golden sands, and inland there are long rows of two-storey concrete buildings, which only look cheerful at night when the big signs for 'Exon' and 'Seafood Snack Shack' and 'Big Daddy's Bar' are lit up.

By daylight the battered cars, the dusty palms and the buildings forever under construction remind you of some half-developed African city – Lagos perhaps, or Ibadan. Florida is called the 'Sunshine State', the temperature is in the 80s, the humidity makes the place feel like the hot-house at Kew and in the summer the mosquitoes remind you of its origins as a swamp. 'People come here,' a judge told me, 'because they expect sun and an easy life. They find unemployment, bad housing and high prices. Then families quarrel and their thoughts turn to murder.' Florida has more of its citizens on Death Row than any other state.

The bay is also handy for South America, which means imports not only of political fugitives but of hashish, heroin, cocaine and qualudes, soothing pills which can be mixed with drink to cause maximum excitement. Even so, there is little evidence of seriously organized crime; the majority of Miami offenders are around twenty years of age, quite often black or Spanish-speaking, most often with a history of drug abuse, frequently armed with knives or easily obtainable firearms, who are brought up to stand their trial before the democratically elected circuit judges of the State Criminal Court, and before the democratically connected eye of the television camera.

It is 150 years since Major Francis L. Dade, who was in fact defeated and killed by the Indians, gave his name to the county. In the courts the severities of frontier justice remain, and almost everyone I met was extremely keen on that stern lady whom politicians, when short of more creative ideas, invoke under the name of Laura Norder. Laura exacts penalties of either death or a minimum twenty-five years without parole for murder, and passes, often through the mouths of women judges, sentences of as much as thirty years on youths guilty of second offences of burglary, the sort of penalty which was only considered appropriate in England for plotting to hand over the vital secrets of our defence to a hostile power.

It is fair to say, however, that if the sentence is served 'cheerfully' and the inmate lends a hand in building more, much-needed prisons, the time may be considerably reduced.

Talbot, known as 'Sandy', D'Alamberte is a prosperous Florida company lawyer with the relaxed good looks of Robert Redford in any film in which he is running for governor. At the top of a high block overlooking the bay, in his offices with their leather sofas, plants, purring telex machines and air-conditioned secretaries (all of which made me remember an English barrister's dusty chambers with peeling law reports and chairs that look like a job lot bought down the Portobello Road), Sandy D'Alamberte relaxed in a white shirt with a bow tie and cotton trousers, and discussed the case he argued in the State Supreme Court for the *Washington Post* and *Newsweek*, which publications have television interests in Florida – the case which confirmed the camera in the courtroom.

There were, of course, precedents, objections and legal arguments. Those opposed to television in court quoted the United States Supreme Court judgements in the case of Billie Sol Estes, a financier whose trial was attended by twelve cameramen and 'cables and wires snaked across the courtroom floor, three microphones were on the judge's bench and others were beamed at the jury box and the counsel's table'. While the defence advocate was arguing for the exclusion of cameras, a cameraman followed him round the court. Chief Justice Warren, when considering this televised trial, was unhappily reminded of the days when 'Premier Fidel Castro conducted his prosecutions before 18,000 people in the Havana Sports Stadium'. However, the Sol Estes case didn't produce a Supreme Court majority against courtroom television. The law and the box became inextricably linked in the case of the *State of Florida* v. *Zamora*.

Young Mr Zamora committed a peculiarly nasty murder, his somewhat hopeless defence being that he had been corrupted by an uninterrupted diet of Kojak and Starsky and Hutch, and programmes which he alleged were criminally negligent of their effect on the minds of psychopaths like him. This television defence was, in fact, fully televised and the jurors in the Zamora case specially asked to be able to watch themselves on the screen in the evenings by way of relaxation after a hard day in court.

Sandy D'Alamberte's opponents put forward strenuous arguments. Television lowers the dignity of the courtoom. It tempts advocates to even more theatrical flourishes. Judges running for election would be afraid to appear 'soft on crime'. Jurors could be recognized in the street by the friends and relatives of those they have convicted and perhaps attacked. Worse still, the arguments continued, a juror's family would say, 'You're not going to let that horrible-looking guy we saw on TV off, are you?' Large portions of the trial go on in the absence of the jury, but all the proceedings would be shown on television and publicized. Witnesses are kept out of court so they can't hear each other's evidence – what use is that if they can see it on the box and trim their words accordingly? Worse perhaps of all, the children of defendants would enter playgrounds where all their fellows had enjoyed, between the cartoons and Charlie's Angels, the shameful spectacle of daddy in the dock.

To these arguments, Sandy D'Alamberte in the Supreme Court of Florida raised powerful democratic answers on behalf of the *Washington Post* which, by virtue of the Great American Tradition of a free press and open government, had toppled President Nixon and exposed the Watergate scandal. If newspapers can report court proceedings, why not TV? If the camera is allowed to see a prisoner hustled down a courtroom corridor, why not see him in court? (Of course the answer to that might be no telly in the corridors; but no one considered such a restriction on press freedom.) Above all, said the advocate for *Post/Newsweek*, this is an open society, we can see congressional committees, we can see the schoolboard discussing sex education in admirably careful and responsible debates through the all-seeing eye in the corner of the living-room. So, if a man may stand for president in that corner, beside the drinks table, under the reproduction Dufy and the fake Polynesian mask, he must be sentenced to death there as well. The Supreme Court of Florida agreed with Sandy D'Alamberte, and now, it seems, only one question remains: should executions also take place in the corner of the living-room?

Mr D'Alamberte, civilized to the tips of his bow tie, is a strong opponent of capital punishment; although his friend, Bob Graham, the young Governor of Florida, has recently signed several death warrants, and John Spenkelink, after a five-year wait on Death Row, was first for the chair. Sandy D'Alamberte argues that executions should be shown on television, so society may be made aware of the barbarities performed in its name, and finally insist that the death penalty be abolished. So, strangely, the most democratic and enlightened arguments, founded on civilized good sense, may lead back to the ten-guinea pub window in Newgate, where the audience thoroughly enjoyed a morning's hanging.

Lance Stelzer, criminal prosecutor of the District Attorney's Office, an undoubted courtroom star, has got perfectly used to cameras in the courtroom; but then Mr Stelzer, as able lawyers must, has grown used to a good deal. Lance Stelzer is a tall, thin young man, wearing the neat three-piece suits and buttoned-down collars favoured by the average reader of *Playboy*. His office contains large but none too healthy plants, and those Escher prints in which endless staircases pursue each other in a world of dizzying optical illusions. He has a girl friend who rings him at work, he does not believe in criminal convictions for those who smoke an occasional joint, and he says, 'If anyone had told me when I was in law school in New York that I would have stood up in court and argued for the death penalty, I'd have told them they were out of their skulls.' Now, moved to the Sunshine State, Lance Stelzer accepts briefs on behalf of death, and argues its powerful case to the jury.

In fact – and here we are back again to the admirable American belief in government by the people for the people – the death penalty is a matter for jury decision and advocates' argument, and not dispassionate judicial sentence. After conviction the jury decides, in a murder case, between the penalties of twenty-five years' minimum imprisonment and death; and their recommendation can be made on a bare majority. It's true that the judge may not accept their recommendation, but the wish of the people, as often as not, is triumphant. Lance Stelzer has a large blown-up card in his office. Down one side are listed the mitigating circumstances in a murder; down the other, and outnumbering them by eight to seven, are the aggravating circumstances which, if found, lead to death. More simply, Mr Stelzer uses the economic argument which has obvious appeal in a monetarist society: 'Why should you and I, members of the jury, pay to keep this clearly worthless man alive for the next twenty-five years?'

In reply, the defence lawyer, having sought in vain for mitigating circumstances, deals with the horrors surrounding 'Old Sparky', as those on Death Row have nicknamed that monument to America's turn-of-the-century pride in technology. The prisoner is prepared, shaved, fed his favourite dishes, through an entire weekend. It takes five minutes to die, in the course of which a victim's blood boils and his eyes are expelled from their sockets. A dead body must be forced from the chair. This spectacle is witnessed by as many as thirty members of the public, and a member of the public volunteers to pull the switch. Government by the people includes an executioner's duties.

'There are so many appeals that no sentence could be carried out in under a year,' Lance Stelzer said to me. 'So it can't possibly be a deterrent.' But he was in court the next day arguing for a death sentence; it is, after all, his job, and he does it extraordinarily well.

The sentence runs: '. . . on such scheduled date you be put to death by having electrical current pass through your body in such amounts and frequency until you are rendered dead' – and these words are periodically pronounced at the end of a murder trial by Judge Lenore C. Nesbitt. Judge Nesbitt is in her forties, has a distinguished civil practice, is married to a probate judge, and is an excellent lawyer and provides a dignified tribunal.

In Judge Nesbitt's court, business is done quickly and efficiently. A boy accused of some violent crime, whose T-shirt bears the legend 'Be nice to your mother', is assigned a public defender; motions are allowed and disallowed with speed and logic. Lady lawyers are asked not to wear open-backed shoes in Judge Nesbitt's court, and defendants chewing gum are offered a sheet of Kleenex from the Bench for its disposal. Judge Nesbitt is against the election of judges and the camera in the courtroom. Television, she thinks, detracts from the dignity of the proceedings, and puts juries under intolerable pressure from their families who will urge them, 'Not to let that evil-looking person off.'

The plants in Judge Nesbitt's office appear healthier than Mr Stelzer's and she lives in a desirable area of Miami. She is not opposed to the death penalty, and in pronouncing its terrible words feels she is part of an endless chain of appeals and the instrument of the jury's, and therefore the people's, will.

'Aw, shit. I'll just get the hell out of here,' said Judge Ellen Morphonios Gable when I telephoned her at the Metro-Justice Building. 'You can meet me out in the country. My husband moved there because of the horses.'

Judge Gable, a blonde with one of the leading roles in the television courtroom saga, has, after a recent divorce, married a Lieutenant Vince Gable of the Department of Public Security. 'Hanging Judge marries Cop' – Vince Gable was proud to tell me what the headlines were, for Judge Ellen rarely awards less than the maximum sentence and has three of her former customers on Death Row.

Her country house is large, not over-tidy – 'I can co-exist with dirt,' said the judge – and its walls are decorated with rifles, shotguns, pistols and Vince's Vietnam medals. 'After eight years in the Marines,' Vince said, 'I only knew work that meant carrying a gun, so I joined the police.' The house has a huge bar, rather like a bleak English pub, with notices reading 'Quiet please, adults at play', and 'Loading bay here'. There is a lot of paddock, a well-built stable and many horses. As I talked to Judge Gable I was nosed by a hefty young Dobermann pinscher which appeared to be wearing a gold medal round its neck, perhaps for bravery in the war against crime.

As a young lawyer, Judge Gable ran a radio chat show called *Lady Ellen*, in which she gave listeners her views on life and the law, and no doubt aired her opinion that the reasons why anyone commits a crime ('So they were deprived when young, were they?') are of no interest to her. She is concerned only, as she says, for the protection of society. Although her sentencing policy does not appear to reduce crime, she is a kind of folk heroine and widely popular.

On the whole, defenders are against television in courtrooms. Frank Rubio is plump, young, still idealistic; repelled by the constant plea bargaining that goes on between judges and most public defenders, he remembers the university professor who told him that everyone has a right to have his case put before a jury, an academic who clearly had little day-to-day experience of American court work.

An older and more cynical defender who has seen it all, from the DA's office and from the judge's Bench, is Alfonso Seppe. He put his feet on the desk in his dark panelled office, with its stereo deck and capacious sofa, and told me that TV has no place in the courtroom. He remembered a murder case in which he was about to cross-examine the victim's wife about her husband's marital infidelities. She objected to the questions as she didn't want her children to see her answering them on TV. So a point of law turned into an argument about what can be shown before the kids go to bed. If the system were exported, we might find evidence being ruled out by Mrs Whitehouse.

However, defending lawyers have an ambivalent attitude to television. Its presence in court often provides the sole ground of appeal.

*

On the day before I left Miami, a Dade County jury was convened to consider whether a boy of twenty who had gone out with a shotgun, wounded two people and finally murdered a store manager for twenty-eight bucks, should die. The judge, Wilkie D. Ferguson Jr, was black, as was the defending counsel and the accused. The judge found out a lot about the potential jurors, what their hobbies were (oil painting, tropical fish, jogging), if they had relatives who were victims of violent crime (one lady's father had been mugged seven times), if they objected to the death penalty on principle (four did) and if they spoke English (six didn't).

After the judge had finished, Lance Stelzer, for the State of Florida, asked a pertinent question: 'If Judge Wilkie D. Ferguson tells you what rules to apply in deciding the issue of life or death,' he said to the jury, 'will you all take his direction, or will you apply to a higher authority, such as, for instance, God?'

One middle-aged woman, after much thought, believed she would take the words of God in preference even to those of Judge Wilkie D. Ferguson Jr. She was asked, most courteously, to leave the court.

'Don't give me Shakespeare!'

DICK FRANCIS
CATHERINE COOKSON
FREDERICK FORSYTH
SHIRLEY CONRAN

DICK FRANCIS

'Who's your favourite writer then?' yelled the taxi driver through his little window. He had discovered that I was in the business.

'I suppose . . . well, I suppose Shakespeare.'

'Shakespeare! Don't give me Shakespeare!' the taxi driver's voice rose to a high pitch of contempt as he cut in neatly in front of the airport bus. 'Artificial characters. *Artificial* bloody characters! Give me Michener every time!'

And give me Michener every time would seem to be the call of readers tramping through the airport bookshops, staggering under the weight of their duty frees, Michener or James Clavell or books which are not books at all but diet sheets, slimming manuals, chronicles of the Brief and Happy Life of Princess Di, Everybody's Book of Deliberate Mistakes, soft-centred erotica by Joan Collins and Anaïs Nin, and a surprising number of works on the subject of rape, volumes which are only seen at airports or in little revolving stands in motels, or in dark corners of shops otherwise devoted to postcards, china starfish and snorkeling equipment. Thousand upon thousand of such works must leave England each summer for foreign beaches, and end up yellowing in the residents' lounge in hotels in Sorrento and Lanzarotte, or expelled from haversacks to make room for a bottle of Valpolicella and a peppered salami.

Not that it is not possible to find, among so many non-books, an occasional work of importance, or at least one which can kill even the longest delay in the stifling departure lounge at Marco Polo airport that modern technology can devise. There is usually, after all, a Graham Greene and a P. G. Wodehouse, there is often a P. D. James, whose novels, if there were any sense in the world, would be on the short-list for the Booker Prize, and as a result of some extremely random selection there is occasionally something quite improbable, like a novel by George Eliot, or a paperback of *The Natural History of Selborne*; and happily, regularly once a year, there is a new Dick Francis.

Mr Francis's work might be said to be perfect holiday reading. He has the true writer's knack of making you want to turn the page, no matter how agonizing you may find such an operation when stretched out on a slab of Aegean rock. He has the magical power of making you forget the sunburn and the mosquito bites, the gyppy tummy and the sickly smell of Ambre Solaire mixed with frying calamaris. He can transport you home to the Berkshire Downs with a string of racehorses exercising in the early morning, or to a small West Country steeplechase where a florid bookmaker with a camel-hair coat and a Bentley is making threatening noises at an unknown jockey who owns little but his broken collar bone, his sense of honour and a mobile home near Didcot.

So as the holidays started, and with his new novel *Banker* about to go under starter's orders, I set out, like an addict seeking out the source of his addiction, to visit Mr Francis.

I found the bungalow as he had described it, next to the dog kennels and with no name on the gate. It was some twenty miles north-east of Lambourn, good training country, and there was nothing about the place which shouted at you, 'World sales of nine million copies.' I knew where I was from the neatness of everything, the sound wooden fences, the lush meadow in which a couple of sleek steeplechasers were turned out. I sat in my car, tired after the long drive through Wallingford. I tried to spell out a life from the back of the Mercedes in the carport to the bush in the white painted tub at the corner of the house. When he came he walked so lightly that I didn't hear his foot on the gravel. He said, 'I'm sorry I was out when you rang.'

Five minutes later Dick Francis was putting a bridle on a mare that stood quietly for him. As he backed it into a horse-box he said, 'Be careful, won't you? The front end bites and the back end kicks.' He is a small man whose round, smiling face looks as if it had been blown and dented like a ping-pong ball by a great slap of wind on a race course. He has been a champion jockey and a war-time pilot and says he has only known fear at the moment when he hands in a manuscript. 'Come and have coffee,' he said. 'Mary's out shopping. She'll be back in a little while.'

'You really weren't afraid riding or flying bombers?'

'I never thought about it. If you can do the job, fear simply doesn't enter into it. When you see the whole line of a racecourse between a horse's ears, it's the most excitin' thing in the world.' Dick Francis clips off his final g's, but in a perfectly classless sort of way. Then he said, in a phrase that echoed the heroic world of Buchan and Bulldog Drummond, 'If you begin to wave the yellow flag your time's up.'

'I was a steeplechase rider for about ten years. You reckon to hit the ground every eleventh or twelfth ride, and remember, you hit it at about thirty miles an hour. Say you have three hundred races a year, that makes almost thirty falls. I've had a fractured skull, six broken collar bones, five broken noses, no end of ribs. Well, you simply stop countin'. The body can't stand that sort of shake-up for more than ten years.

'Is racing really crooked? Steeplechasing much less than flat racin', and even so it's not nearly so crooked in real life as in my books. A jockey can't bet, which is where the dicey possibilities are. That's why the bookmakers are the baddies in my books. Sometimes a trainer will get together with a jockey and they'll decide to hold back a good horse who's heavily handicapped for a number of races. Then, when the handicap's been lowered and his price lengthens, the trainer will have a lot of money laid about the horse and they'll let it win. That never happened in the stables I rode for as a professional. I rode for Lord Bicester and then for Peter Cazalet who trained the Queen Mother's horses.

'My father was a steeplechase jockey before the First World War, then he became a horse-dealer near Maidenhead. Mother brought us up strictly and I'm sure it did us good. Father thought a day out huntin' taught you much more than a day at school. My son trains at Lambourn and I'm happy to go out early in the morning and lead out his string on the Downs. I still like to feel the wind in my face provided it isn't too cold. What do I hate? I detest snobbery and people who turn up late. I always used to get to the racecourse at least an hour too early just to get the feeling of the place.

'I start writin' a new book on 1 January each year and I deliver the manuscript to my publisher on 8 May. One year Mary was very ill and her mother died and I was two weeks late.'

If Dick Francis's baddies are bookmakers, his heroes are often jockeys, with a code of honour as stoical as that of Philip Marlow. They have been round some pretty mean racetracks, and drive rather old motor-cars. Their ways are spartan, and their idea of a feast is a plate of bacon and eggs and a cup of strong tea after a long fast. Their bodies are broken by falls, or by the bully-boys employed by scheming bookies or egomaniac owners. The good are wiry and down to ten stone, the bad are florid and overweight. Sex is fairly frequent, but it has a certain innocence and is even accompanied by love. There is a good deal of decency in Dick Francis's books, and it even extends to his villains, who rarely try to kill their heroes but seem content with locking them up in horseboxes and twisting their broken limbs for them.

From the stable lad in his converted trailer to the manipulating owner in his smugly rich spread in the Home Counties, the author has a minute eye for detail. He also has the advantage of being able to introduce the reader to a country for which he has all the maps, a fascinating world of genetics and veterinary practice and greed and obsession and the courage of weather-beaten flyweights who balance half a ton of horse with instinctive precision and send it hurtling over enormous obstacles to a small present for the winner or the orthopaedic hospital for one in ten.

'You gave up being a jockey when you were thirty-six?'

'Yes. I'd had ten years at the top . . . and there was the business of Devon Loch.'

Devon Loch was Dick Francis's great disappointment, something, I imagine, not even four million readers will make up for. It was the supreme moment of his career, jumping the last fence at Aintree and going away ten lengths ahead of the opposition, a horse called ESB. He was riding the Queen Mother's horse, the Queen and her mother were watching the race, and Devon Loch with Dick Francis up was to be his, and her, first Grand National winner. No one quite knows what happened, and he thinks it was the sudden crescendo of cheering from the enthusiastic crowd which hit the horse an almost physical blow. At any rate, just thirty yards from the winning-post, Devon Loch sank on her hind quarters and, having pulled a muscle in doing so, couldn't recover to win the race. Dick Francis walked away from the track in bitter disappointment, although he won races on the mysteriously afflicted horse after that.

'After my next injury (I had a broken wrist) the Queen Mother's racin' adviser said perhaps I should get out while I was at the top. So I did. I didn't want to be a trainer. I had half an autobiography written, the story of a jockey, and I was asked to write some articles for the *Daily Express*. I began to look at the holes in the carpet and think of the boys' education. Mary said, "Why not write a novel? I'll help on the English." She'd been to university, you know, and she was a stage manager at the local theatre. We had a regular seat at the New Theatre, Oxford, and we used to go when I came back from racing in the Midlands. I suppose I was the only jockey who went to the theatre once a week. Jockeys are mostly farmers' sons, or small-sized boys from the back streets of northern towns.'

'You'd never written anything before?'

'Only letters home, when I was with the RAF in Africa. I used to describe everything in my letters and people seemed to enjoy them.'

'What had you read, when you were a boy?'

'I read Bulldog Drummond, of course . . . and Edgar Wallace. I read Nat Gould's racing stories, but they were mainly about betting.'

I marvelled how a talent for fiction could be discovered in middle age, born of nothing much, it seemed, but an instinctive taste for seeing a line of obstacles clearly between the quivering ears of a racehorse.

Mary Francis came back from shopping and her husband poured the drinks from a cupboard in the long, airy sitting room, looking out on the garden and the paddock beyond. She's fair-haired, smiling and motherly and looks after his business affairs. When he wrote *Reflex*, she took up photography to help him with the technical knowledge and now has a darkroom fixed up in their loo. For one book Mr and Mrs Francis flew to Italy with a plane load of nervous racehorses, and brought another consignment back on the same day.

'What about morality?' I said. 'In *Banker* the hero's passionately in love with a married woman, and she loves him, but despite all the opportunities they're given, they don't sleep together until after her husband dies, rather conveniently, of a cerebral haemorrhage on the last page.'

'We asked four friends about that,' said Mary Francis, 'two married and two unmarried, and they all agreed that Dick's characters shouldn't go to bed together while the husband was still alive, no matter how much they wanted to.'

'But in *Forfeit*, where the racing journalist's wife has polio and is on a life support machine, and he meets this wonderful black girl called Gail who makes love to him on a fluffy white rug in her uncle's house in Virginia Water . . .'

'*Coloured* girl,' Dick corrected me gently.

'Well, at the end the wife finds out, after the baddies have kidnapped her, and she says that he can sleep with Gail regularly on Thursdays provided he always comes home.' In fact it's a touching ending, and one which must make most readers long for the simple life with such sensible solutions. 'Would you have minded,' I asked Mary, who had been, for one brief and terrifying period of their lives, in an iron lung after an attack of polio, 'if Dick . . . ?'

'If one was a *permanent* invalid,' Mary drew the clear distinction. 'A *permanent* invalid couldn't really expect the other partner . . . I was never an invalid,' she ended firmly, 'for very long.'

Finally I asked Dick Francis how he would define the strong sense of morality which underlies his marvellously told racing stories.

'What it comes to,' he said, 'is that I never ask my main character to do anything I wouldn't do myself.'

CATHERINE COOKSON

Going up to Newcastle on what may have been the last train out of King's Cross I looked towards that remote countryside where the fifteen-year-old Katie Mulholland hid behind a curtain in the rich mine-owner's house where she worked as a scullery maid. Katie had only wanted to watch the ball, but the intolerable Bernard Rosier, the young master, found her and carried her, without a by-your-leave, into his big feather bed and then, unhappily:

> Her limbs flailed wildly until a weight fell on her body and Hell opened and engulfed her . . . He had taken her without the slightest endearment, not even bothering to caress her limbs, which courtesy he bestowed on the meanest of women. He had taken her with less feeling than a dog would a bitch, and he hadn't deigned to open his mouth to her from beginning to end.

Katie Mulholland is, of course, sacked when she becomes pregnant, but despite this unfortunate start in life lives on through some 406 pages, through her father's execution for murdering her husband, through incest in the family, further rape in the family, through the unwanted friendship of a lesbian feminist and a short spell in the nick on a trumped-up charge of keeping a disorderly house, to die in an air raid at the age of ninety-eight and become the heroine of one of the best of Catherine Cookson's novels, fifty-six of which have sold around 40 million copies.

On my journey into the land of Catherine Cookson and Katie Mulholland I travelled through a beautiful stretch of the Tyne to Hexham. Then I was met by Tom Cookson, who got to know his wife when he was a schoolmaster in Hastings and she was supervising the laundry in the local workhouse.

'Yes, they called them workhouses then,' Tom said as he drove me towards the Cheviots, over country where there had once been lead and silver mines, to a stone house by a man-made lake, dug for smelting the lead. 'We used to live near the main road to Scotland,' he said, 'but so many people used to ring the bell and peer over the fence to see Catherine you dared not go near the windows. So we moved here, into the wilds.'

He also explained his wife's illness, which meant they had to live near a doctor they trusted. So I expected to meet a frail old lady of seventy-six, worn out by an exhausting complaint and the effort of writing so many books.

In fact I found a remarkably lively, red-haired woman who laughed a great deal, spoke with a trace of an Irish accent, and led me into a room which looked like nothing more than a small antechamber in the Palace of Versailles, full of glittering chandeliers, chintz sofas and eighteenth-century portraits.

'We converted this room,' Mrs Cookson said, as though it were the most natural thing in the world, 'out of an old swimming pool. Now then, what do you want to ask me?'

'Suppose we start at the beginning,' I said, in all innocence. 'What was your father like?'

The author of *Katie Mulholland* laughed for quite a long time. Then she said, 'I wish to God I knew!'

Of course, I should have known better.

*

The great strength of Catherine Cookson's writing lies in her descriptions of nineteenth-century industrial society. She can re-create the shipyards and coal mines of the North-East, the back streets of Jarrow and South Shields in the 1880s. She knows the smell of excrement in the dark tenement rooms, the rare comfort of a black pudding, the brutality of slum streets which their inhabitants missed so desperately when they were offered fresh air and a house in the country. Her books have a great value for the information they contain, and their strong feeling for social injustice. This is Mrs Cookson on a nineteenth-century colliery weighman:

> Mark Bunting . . . the 'keeker' as he was called by the men, was the man who checked the corves of coal hewed by the miners; he was the man who had the power to cut a man's wages by as much as half if the seven-hundredweight basket the miner sent up from the black bowels of the earth should show a deficiency of two or three pounds. Often when this happened all the coal in the basket was made free to the owner. No account was taken for the men having to get the coal out, even by the light of a candle. The keekers worked on a commission basis, the more corves they found faulty and could pass as free to the owners, the more money they themselves made.

If Catherine Cookson's stories sound melodramatic, many a servant girl in nineteenth-century England did live a life of melodrama, always liable to be seduced by her employer and thrown on to the streets when she got pregnant. The strength of the poor is genuine in Catherine Cookson's books because she was a little girl in Jarrow, the daughter of 'Our Kate', a larger-than-life character given to alternate bouts of affection and drunken rage, with an Irish grandad who, 'Didn't drink, he bathed in the stuff and thought Hell was reserved for Protestants.' She walked the streets with the 'grey hen', a big jug of beer for her mother, or picked up the bits of coal that fell off the carts. She counted herself lucky to be able to leave service, which she hated, and get a job in the workhouse laundry.

★

We sat under the chandeliers and Mrs Cookson talked fast as though she had a great deal to say and far too little time in which to say it.

'Neighbours said they'd seen my father and told me, "Your Da was a gentleman. He wore an astrakhan collar and kid gloves. He carried a silverheaded walking stick and talked lovely." Of course, he never married "Our Kate".

'It makes me mad when I see these well-off ladies having about three gins before dinner and then four glasses of wine, and maybe a liqueur, and Kate only had to sniff a whisky and she'd go out of her head.

'What did I read when I was a child? The woman upstairs gave me Grimm's fairy tales. And then I read romantic novels, Ethel M. Dell and Elinor Glyn. I'm eternally grateful to Elinor Glyn. There was a book of hers where a secretary was going to marry a duke and she had to learn to be a lady, so she read *Lord Chesterfield's Letters to His Son*. I wanted to be a lady very badly too, so I read Lord Chesterfield. He helped me enormously, my life's really been Lord Chesterfield *versus* my Grand-da. Then I went to the public library and read all sorts of things, Erasmus and John Donne and Chaucer. At first I thought Erasmus made that "Erathmic Soap" they used to advertise, but I soon learnt better. I never read Hardy and I thought Dickens's writing was too elaborate.

'Lord Chesterfield took me in hand and I began to talk proper. I used to write plays about dukes and duchesses, things I knew nothing at all about. They made game of me in the workhouse laundry. They teased me and made me apple-pie beds.

'It was terrible in the workhouse. Married couples used to come in and be given these stamped clothes and then parted at once. Women had to stay fourteen years in there, until their kids grew up. I had the job of taking them up to the children's home to visit once a month. That was where I learnt compassion.

'I wrote some stories and sent them up to a "literary school" that advertised in the paper. They came back with the comment, "We strongly advise this author not to take up writing as a career."

'My Grand-da was a Catholic, but the Catholic Church seems to threaten you all the time. I've got no use for the fear of God and now I'm an agnostic. But I think about God a lot of the time and sometimes I feel as religious as a whole busload of nuns. I'm not interested in politics at all.'

'Don't your feelings about the exploitation of the miners, for instance, make you political?'

'Not at all. I'm too busy looking for God to look for an MP.'

'How would you describe your books?'

'I don't think I'm a romantic writer. I think I write social histories of the North.'

'But there's quite a lot of sex in your novels.'

'The only sort of four-letter words I use are "good", "love", "warm" and "kind". But, of course, sex happens. I dictate everything into a machine now, and my secretary comes on Mondays to collect the tapes. I rang her up yesterday to ask her where I'd got to in a book and she said, "Oh, Mrs Cookson, you've just got to the bit where they're doing naughties in the wood." '

The young Catherine Cookson moved south and took over the laundry in the Hastings workhouse. There are photographs of her at the time, a very pretty girl in the early 1930s, who by some extraordinary effort of will, managed to save enough money to buy a 'fifteen-roomed gentleman's residence' which she turned into a hostel for mental defectives. She also met the young schoolmaster who became her husband.

After her marriage to Tom, Catherine Cookson suffered four miscarriages and a nervous breakdown which involved some horrific ECT treatment. She has described the terrors of that time movingly and listed her collection of fears: 'Fear of God. Fear of loving and slipping the way of Kate. Fear of people and what they might say about my having no Da. Fear of losing Tom in the war, a great consuming, agonizing fear. Fear of the priest and of his admonitions from behind the grid in the confessional. Fear of swear-words, this was with me always.'

Happily Mrs Cookson emerged from these dark days and took to writing novels. And Tom is with her always, cooking, driving and typing the answers to the 3,000 letters she gets a year, many from people suffering from her strange fear of being ostracized for being born out of wedlock. 'It's men that feel it most,' she says in a phrase that has the true ring of her period, the nineteenth century. 'A man can't stand the idea that his mother was an impure woman.'

We talked about her dreams, and Mrs Cookson told me that she often dreamed about lavatories, which she took to be a good sign because such dreams usually heralded a large cheque from her publisher. In fact she has found that the dirtier the toilet facilities in her dreams the larger the cheque that follows. She had dreams of being sent to prison.

'Do you think about going to prison?' she asked me.

'A lot. It's one of my fears also.'

'There you are, you see. And we haven't done anything wrong. What it must be like for those actually in prison I can't imagine. I think of them so much. Their suffering must be terrible.'

Catherine Cookson is the only person out of the many I have interviewed who seems to have spent any time at all worrying about the condition of prisoners. But then she learnt her compassion in a hard school.

*

What do these two hugely popular authors have in common, apart from the unmistakable talent for knowing how to make the reader turn the pages and their meticulous eye for detail? They both took to writing novels comparatively late in life, in their thirties, after a great deal of hard-won experience which provides their material and after some personal disaster. Dick Francis walked away from the collapse of Devon Loch and Catherine Cookson emerged from the hospital that smelled of urine and the appalling electric shocks, the black hole of depression, to become a best-seller. There is something else. They are both good people, writers whose reactions to the world are consistently decent, tolerant and humane. It is this, I am sure, that earns them the affection of so many readers. If many of the paper-backs that flow in a great tide from the airports to the beaches this summer are non-books, that disparaging phrase could never be used of a work by a Dick Francis or a Catherine Cookson.

'You don't write artificial characters,' the taxi driver who took me to the airport said. 'Not like bloody Shakespeare. In fact I'd put you right up there with Michener.'

Choking back my rage, I tipped the man and then slunk off to the bookstall, just to check whether I was on the shelves.

FREDERICK FORSYTH

A pattern emerges in the lives of the best-selling novelists. Many are not, it seems, born writers; they achieve writing or have it thrust upon them. It happens comparatively late in life and after a successful other career, as a steeplechase jockey, or as the manageress of a workhouse laundry, or, in the case of Frederick Forsyth, as a foreign correspondent. Then comes some disaster, the loss of a job, a nervous breakdown, a horse that unaccountably sits down when in the lead thirty yards from the winning post at Aintree. A new career is needed, it's almost as if it's too late for anything but a success. Mr Forsyth didn't start writing fiction until he was in his thirties; it took him exactly four years to become a millionaire.

There is also a pattern in the books, which partly explains their compulsive readability. A plot that may be improbable is presented with great confidence and a minute attention to realistic detail; the surface is so convincing that the reader's belief is retained as the story soars into melodrama. You close the book convinced that beneath the surface of every-day life extraordinary adventures are still possible: this is a thought which brings great comfort to the average reader on the 9.30 charter flight from Gatwick.

The technique is, of course, as old as the dawn of story telling. You only have to consider this passage:

> Telemachus threw open the door of his comfortable room, sat down on the bed and took off his soft tunic, which he put in the wise old woman's hands. After folding and smoothing it out, she hung it on a peg by the wooden bedstead, and withdrew from the bedroom, pulling the door to by the silver handle and shooting the bolt by means of its leather thong. And there, all the night long, under his woollen blanket Telemachus lay planning in his mind the journey that Athene had prescribed.

Homer knew that after that sort of detail the readers would have no difficulty in accepting the whole of the Circe story. It would come as no surprise to read of Telemachus getting up, putting on a Sulka dressing gown over his Turnbull & Asser pyjamas and ordering fresh orange juice, wholewheat toast and lightly scrambled eggs. On arrival in Pylos he might take a Martini, stirred and not shaken.

'Turn right off the motorway, three quarters of a mile to the village, right a thousand yards to the pub, left a thousand yards to a sign held up by two posts, and then at a hundred and fifty yards . . .'

The instructions were so clipped and rapid that I expected the final command to be, 'Fire!' Instead the voice over the telephone said, 'My house.'

My mind was full of Frederick Forsyth's *The Devil's Alternative* which I had been reading in preparation for this mission into Surrey. I knew the dimensions of the room in which the Politburo meets in the Arsenal of the Kremlin (about fifty feet long and twenty-five feet wide). I knew that in the Oval Office the President of the United States sits with his back to the south wall of the room, facing northward towards the classical marble fireplace. I suspected that, owing to the failure of the Russian grain harvest, a power struggle in the Kremlin and the misguided zeal of certain Ukrainian freedom fighters, the Third World War was about to break out. I marvelled that this possibility, the continuing nightmare of our age, should make such enormously popular reading.

The directions were meticulously accurate. At exactly one hundred and fifty yards past the sign I turned into the driveway of a large white house surrounded by rose beds and manicured lawns. I saw a lily pond and a children's swing. A thin man dressed in white came out to greet me. It was, as Frederick Forsyth might say at the end of a chapter, 'Just half past ten in Surrey, and going to be a warm day.'

'My father went to Malaya to plant rubber. He didn't prosper and came back to join my mother in her furrier's business in Dartford. The wireless was always on when I was a child. What did I read? Oh, *Just William*, Buchan and Henty, Leslie Charteris and Jeffrey Farnol. I hadn't much time for Bulldog Drummond. I loved Rider Haggard.'

'Umslopogas!' I said, thinking no writer of adventure stories could have a better model. 'And Captain Good with his monocle and his full-dress naval uniform in a tin box.'

'And the "woodpecker", Umslopogas's little war axe he just tapped his enemies on the head with. The trouble was, the Masai were always the heavies in Rider Haggard, and really the Masai are such kind, gentle people.'

'Did you want to be a writer?'

'Not at all. I wanted to be a fighter pilot or a foreign correspondent. My father read the *Daily Express*, which used to be full of reports from "our man on the spot", Sefton Delmer or René MacColl, and then he would get out the atlas and show me where the trouble-spots were. And, of course, father had been to the Orient, he told me about tiger shoots and the head-hunters of Borneo.

'I went to Tonbridge, where most of the old boys leave to join the Stock Exchange. They told me then that I shouldn't be a journalist and that reporters were grubby little fellows with dirty macs, forever drinking cups of cold tea. I asked them if they thought that the editor of *The Times* was like that and they had to concede that he wasn't.'

'But you didn't go into journalism at once?'

'No. I left Tonbridge at seventeen and signed on with the RAF. I had six months to kill, so I went to Spain. I'd always been good at languages at school. I was rather small and my way of keeping in with other boys was to do their French and German prep for them.

'I went to the University of Granada, but I didn't do much studying. I'd read Hemingway and I followed Ordoñez round the bullfights. Then I used to go to the bullrings in the morning with a crowd of Spanish teenagers. We practised passes, not with real bulls. They were far too expensive, so we used to pay a couple of urchins to run across the sand with bull horns fixed on perambulators and we fought them manfully.

'I went into the RAF in May 1956 and enjoyed it. But I didn't want to sign on for another twelve or twenty-two years. I'd got my wings and then I decided to try my other career. I joined the *Eastern Daily Press* and began the great adventure of reporting cage-bird shows from King's Lynn.'

We were in a room that might have belonged to one of the Surrey stockbrokers the masters of Tonbridge wanted Freddie Forsyth to be. There was an expanse of carpet, two large arm chairs, an open fireplace, English landscapes with lights over them on the walls, the Forsyth novels bound in leather and some other writers, Kipling and Oscar Wilde. Mr Forsyth talked well, with a certain irony and the volubility of an only child ('I was an only child,' he told me, 'which is why I'm never lonely.'). Now and again his small son staggered into the room to be greeted, and expelled, with courtesy. When the telephone rang the call was from Nigeria, to which country Mr Forsyth's great hero General Ojuku has now returned to a popular welcome. Frederick Forsyth still keeps up his friendship with the former Biafran leader and wanted to let him know that the Ojuku children has departed safely for their school holidays with their father.

'I had a good three years in Norfolk. I had an MG and lots of girl friends. Then I wore out my shoe leather walking up and down

Fleet Street until I managed to get into Reuters because of my languages. I went to the Paris office in May 1962. I had no wife, no children, no possessions except a bed-sitting room in Bayswater. Paris was a great place for a young man to be. It was the time of the OAS emergency. Lots of bombs, in fact there was *plasticage* almost every day.

'I had the job of following de Gaulle around to see if he got his head blown off. I began to chat to his bodyguards, who were all extremely tough Corsicans. There are long periods of boredom and waiting around in the life of a bodyguard, and they were quite pleased to talk to me. Then, around September 1963, I heard a rumour in a bar that the OAS were going to hire an outsider to kill de Gaulle, because they'd been frustrated so many times. I suppose that put the idea of *The Day of the Jackal* into my subconscious, but it stayed there doing nothing for the next six years. In those days in Paris I still didn't have any idea that I could ever write a novel.'

In 1967, the events started which were to prove the turning point in the life of Frederick Forsyth. He had joined the BBC news, and despite his protests that he was a dedicated European, it was decided to send him to Nigeria. The BBC and the Foreign Office told him that the Biafran War was a little bush uprising which would be over in ten days, and that Ojuku had no popular support and no legitimate complaint against the Nigerian government.

'When I got there I found I'd been given a load of cod. There was a long and bloody war in the brew, the people had been savagely mistreated; Ojuku was an articulate, highly intelligent man who was generally idolized. I sent back reports which told the truth about Biafra, and about the starving children and the appalling suffering. Unknown to me, the British High Commissioner in Lagos flew home to complain about my reports. I was recalled and told I'd never be sent abroad again. In fact I was dispatched to Siberia, which meant reporting Parliament. I don't think that did me any good, except to dispel any lingering faith I might have had in the wisdom of our elected leaders.

'No more true news was coming out of Biafra, there was only mangled news from Lagos. I was still being accused of having slanted the news in favour of Ojuku, so I quit.'

But even then he didn't write a book, but returned to Biafra, the world of gun-running and mercenaries and babies as starving, feverish bundles concealed in the bush by nuns. It was a world he was to use to stunning effect six years later in *The Dogs of War*, a book that is, on any showing, a marvellous adventure story, and I think a very good novel.

'I took a flight to Lisbon,' Mr Forsyth remembered. 'I asked some questions in a bar and found an American gun-runner who took me to Biafra with two crates of mortars in an old Constellation. I was recognized, the BBC was pretty unpopular there then, and I was nearly arrested as a spy. I went to see Ojuku and told him that I'd quit my job and asked him if I could write some articles. He raised an elegant eyebrow and said, "Who for?" "Oh, things like *Time* magazine," I said hopefully. In fact I wrote for *Time*, the *Evening Standard* and the *Daily Express*. I was there for two years, while a million people died. I was accused of being an arms trafficker and Ojuku's personal adviser. There was even a story that I ran a group of mercenaries like those in *The Dogs of War*. I tell you, tales of my wickedness have been greatly exaggerated.

'The war ended and Ojuku had to flee the country. I had to make a bob or two. I'd bought a lot of supposed thrillers, paperbacks at airports. They were illogical stories on which no trouble had been taken. I thought, "I'll write a book and make a little money quickly." In fact it took quite a long time to make a lot.'

He wrote *The Day of the Jackal* in thirty-five days at the start of 1970. It was turned down by four publishers, who all thought there could be no suspense in a plot about the assassination of de Gaulle when everyone knew that the general was still alive and living in Colombey-les-deux-Églises. Then Freddy Forsyth came to the conclusion that the publishers weren't really reading his book, so he wrote a twenty-page synopsis. Finally, Harold Harris of Hutchinson read the book over a week-end and accepted it at once.

Bantam Books in America paid the largest advance ever paid for a first novel, one of $365,000. 'It was a case of "*The Day of the* What? by Fred *Who*?" ' says Mr Forsyth, but the book gathered momentum. It, and his other three major novels, have together now sold around 10 million copies.

'I make myself write a long day. I do twelve pages because I really hate writing. And I honestly don't care too much about the money. I live in England now, and I'm quite content to pay English tax.'

'If you don't like the writing or the money, what do you enjoy?'

'I love the research. I got all the details for *The Devil's Alternative* from Soviet dissidents who'd made it to the West and were in touch with American academics. I did six months' research for that book, in America, Oslo, Rotterdam, Amsterdam, Berlin and Moscow. I did a day in the dacha country and found the restaurant where the British agent Munro meets his contact called "The Nightingale". I spent a day in the Kremlin and got a ground plan of it. When I'm researching a novel, I'm like a journalist chasing a story. I find it enormously exciting.'

I remembered Dick Francis and Catherine Cookson and the simple morality, the triumph of the good in their stories. I asked Frederick Forsyth about his own sense of morality, which is clearly more complex.

'I like to write about immoral people doing immoral things. I want to show that the Establishment's as immoral as the criminals.'

'Are you at all political?'

'No. I can't really manage deeply held beliefs. I respect the passionate commitment of Mrs Thatcher or Michael Foot, but I can't honestly share in it.'

'Do you think we'll have a nuclear war? I was scared to death by *The Devil's Alternative*.'

'No. I think we'll have lots of little proxy wars, with the superpowers lining up behind each side. There won't be a holocaust, but it'll end in a line of weariness and chaos, as it has in Africa.'

'Or Lebanon?'

'Exactly.'

I thought of the words of the mercenary in *The Dogs of War*, the man who sees war for what it is, a brutal business of killing with no spurious idealism attached:

> The ones back home who cheer for war 'We're always right and they're always wrong' . . . They're being conned. Those GIs in Vietnam, do you think they died for life, liberty and the pursuit of happiness? They died for the Dow Jones Index in Wall Street, and always have done. And the British soldiers who died in Kenya, Cyprus, Aden. You really think they rushed into battle shouting for God, King and Country? They were in those lands because their Colonel ordered them there, and he was ordered by the War Office and that was ordered by the Cabinet to keep British control over their economies . . . It's a big con, Julie Manson, a big con. The difference with me is that no one tells me which side to fight on . . .

The cynicism may not be complete, however. *The Dogs of War* ends with the establishment of a government under a benevolent general, who seems not a million miles removed from Ojuku.

'What are you going to write next?' I asked Freddie Forsyth.

'I don't know. It's a bit of a problem. When you've been writing about the struggle between Washington and the Kremlin it's a bit hard to do a novel about a pay-roll robbery from a dairy in East Acton.'

It was 12.30 p.m. on a hot day in Surrey when I turned out of Mr Forsyth's drive. World War Three had not yet broken out.

SHIRLEY CONRAN

After a moment's thought Kate fished a notebook out of her cigar-brown Gucci tote-bag, did as Judy said, then tore off the page and handed it to her.

Judy beamed. 'Great. Now expand those three sentences into a synopsis and split it up into chapters. And I'll let you practise being a famous author by taking you out to supper . . .' The following evening Judy fiddled around with Kate's synopsis, altered the pagination slightly and then said, 'Fine. This I can promote . . .'

The characters, of course, are entirely fictional and their businesslike approach to the world of letters comes from a new block-buster due to land at Heathrow in time for the September holidays, and at transatlantic airports somewhat earlier. *Lace* has already earned its author, Shirley Conran (whose domestic handbook *Superwoman* has sold around a million copies), half a million pounds for the book rights and another half a million for an American television production. It is a work which traces, over some 599 pages, the lives of a group of girls who started together in a Swiss finishing school; an establishment which includes, among the social obstacles provided, the risk of being handcuffed to a bed by the headmaster's chauffeur and photographed in compromising positions for the purposes of blackmail. The story also concerns a devastating young film actress who calls the old school friends to a meeting in the Plaza Hotel, New York, for the purpose of asking the book's vital question: 'Which of you bitches is my mother?' The assorted lovers described include a handsome Sheik named Abdullah who says he has 'a restless spirit', an elderly Greek shipping tycoon who interrupts dinner with lines like, 'Get Amsterdam on the telex and check the bauxite price', a boy of fifteen and a New York publisher called Griffin Lowe with winged black eyebrows. The story zips from one sexual encounter to another without a dull moment, and the varied settings will no doubt make a nice change from Texas. Curious to discover what it felt like to write your first novel in middle life and make a cool million before you've sold a single copy, I travelled to the South of France to visit the 'Superwoman' in person.

Monte Carlo must be the ultimate penalty for the successful writer. The high-rise blocks glower over the strip of gritty beach; it is a place in which the heart cries out for the old-world charm of Blackpool. I met Mrs Conran in the bar of the local Trusthouse Forte as last orders were being called and an army of dripping children staggered up from the pool to invade the lifts. It was there, on the Avenue Princesse Grace, that Shirley Conran let me into the secret of how she came to write a money-spinner.

'I was determined to reach the American best-seller list. I didn't need to be top, but I had to be *in* it. And I thought, what's the thing that will do it this year, and I said, "Incest." I decided to try it with one book, and if that wasn't going to make money I'd stop. I mean, I didn't know if I could write a novel at all. What do I read? I read Tolstoy, and when I read *Hadji-Murad* I was arguing with Tolstoy because I think his story would have been much better edited and if he'd cut five chapters. I think I'd like Thackeray to read my book. Oh, when I was going to write it I read the life of Virginia Wade. It's her tenacity I admire, keeping at it until you win. I was at St Paul's with Shirley Williams, and I think they taught you tenacity there, you had to keep going to stay third or fourth in the class. You couldn't get higher than that because some of the girls had photographic memories.

'I have a wonderful editor at Simon & Schuster in New York – Michael Korda. He blue-pencilled my literary pretensions. I didn't realize how much education I'd picked up. He was always asking, "Is this page going to bore a truck driver?" He says I'm a natural, and of course that gave me self-confidence.'

Mrs Conran is a still beautiful woman who speaks in a husky voice and sits with her face tilted upwards in an attitude of nervous courage. Her father, who prospered in the dry-cleaning business, was given, she told me, to violent drunken rages. 'He wasn't poor. Oh no. He left mother his last Rolls-Royce. I left St Paul's and went to a finishing school in Switzerland, not at all like the one in the book. Then I went to an art school in Portsmouth. I had an exhibition at the Architectural Association when I was twenty-one. It was a sell-out.'

Then Shirley Conran walked into a coffee bar owned by Terence Conran, then a young furniture designer. 'When I married Terence I ran his showroom. I had the same natural facility for PR and entertaining as I have for writing.' Mr Conran became the hugely successful originator of the Habitat empire and Mrs Conran wrote for and edited the women's pages of a number of newspapers and magazines. When their marriage broke up she said she found that money, which she had never thought much about, became important when you didn't have it. So she wrote *Superwoman*, which she thinks owes its huge success to the fact that it gave women permission not to do the housework. ('Don't sew,' the business-like Superwoman advises. 'Mend sheet tears with press-on tape. Stick patches on with Copydex.')

'Tell me about the sex scenes in your book. Are they there because all block-busters have them?'

'Not really. I wrote them because I wanted to show that D. H. Lawrence got it *wrong*, and Hemingway got it *wrong*. They didn't understand how women feel.'

In *Lace*, Judy has a lunch-time rendezvous with Griffin Lowe. After a snack at the bedside (smoked trout and half a bottle of Pouilly Fumé) the publisher dresses to return to a hard day at his office. The incensed Judy ties her lover to the bed, gags him with her tights, makes love to him and then goes to the kitchen for a pair of 'shears' with which she cuts up his hand-made suit and slashes his shirt specially imported from Jermyn Street. Finally she pours olive oil and a highball over him, grinds a lemon-meringue pie into his face and goes to the office herself, leaving the unhappy Griffin like the remains of a cookery demonstration.

'I suppose I can imagine a girl feeling like that, when her married lover dresses for an urgent appointment with the managing director. But you've never *done* such a thing, have you?'

'Oh no.' Mrs Conran smiled. 'I'm very straight. Michael Korda said the scene was physically impossible. But finally we found someone who agreed to do it to her husband when they went to stay with his mother in the country. It worked perfectly well.'

'Is your book written for women?'

'I know how women react. I'm good at that. It's written for women about men. I suppose about 30 per cent of the readers may be men who read it to find out about women.'

'It seems strange to me to divide your audience by their sex. Are women readers really so different from men readers?'

'Of course. Men can't have babies. They don't cook.'

'They cook. In huge numbers, surely.'

'Not every day, so it keeps coming back, like onions. I want to tell women it's no use relying on other people. You've got to go out and do it yourself – earn a quarter of a million dollars or start a business.'

Mrs Conran was about to leave for a promotional tour for her book. *Lace* contains helpful advice to the promoting author whose great misfortune is to lose her 'television wardrobe' at the airport. As Judy says, all you really need are 'a couple of lightweight dresses for the South and for the evenings and one good suit with at least seven blouses because you won't have time to wash one out every night . . . and get some junk jewellery and scarves . . . Margot Fonteyn tours with . . . just one black suit. In between interviews she sits in the back of the limo, turns the collar up or down, pulls some pearls or a scarf out of her tote-bag and manages six entirely different looks in one day.'

In spite of some exotic sex, *Lace* seems to recall the old world of romantic fiction. Read a sentence like, 'Then he gently pulled off her sheer black panty hose and laid her, still trembling, on the yielding soft cushions of the couch,' and you're back in the great days of Elinor Glyn on the tigerskin rug.

I remembered how Miss Glyn's work had inspired Catherine Cookson, because a secretary in one of her romantic novels had been advised to read Lord Chesterfield's letters to prepare her for marriage to a duke. Miss Cookson then herself read Lord Chesterfield and her literary interests were awakened.

Perhaps becoming a best-selling author is the modern equivalent to a ducal marriage, and I wondered if some mute, inglorious Catherine Cookson might get similar help from *Lace*. Anyone who reads it will find much useful advice on perfume ('Diorissima' gets high marks), interior decoration ('Zebra skins lay on the dark, hardwood floor and an antique, red-and-black painted Persian screen zig-zagged across one corner'), how to behave with sang-froid in the presence of the great ('You can't be late at your own reception . . . when the Nixons are the guests of honour'; 'I came with the Javitses but I don't think they're staying'; 'Nobody can fix Buckingham Palace . . . Christopher suggested about a year ago that you might be welcome because of the work you've done for Cancer Research'), and eating on aeroplanes ('Maxine had merely accepted a little caviar, no toast, and only one glass of champagne, non-vintage but Moët she observed, with approval before accepting it. From a burgundy suede tote-bag she had then produced a small white plastic box that contained a small silver spoon, a pot of home-made yoghurt and a large, juicy peach from her own hot-house'). However, having gone through all of *Lace*'s many pages, I found no mention of *Lord Chesterfield's Letters to His Son*. It is, I suppose, a book much out of fashion now, and no one could ever say of it, 'This I can promote!'

The Lost Leader

DENIS HEALEY

'Keith Joseph?' said the voice across the dinner table. 'A wonderful mixture of Rasputin and Tommy Cooper.'

I looked and there was Denis Healey, red-faced, beetle-browed, as recognizable as Mike Yarwood or John Bull, one of the few politicians who seems able to make a joke or who will take a huge diversion on a drive to a political meeting to add to his considerable collection of rare books, or who can talk with equal authority on monetarism, opera or the early Russian cinema. The conversation turned to William Blake, of whom his knowledge is profound. So, I thought, it might be interesting to learn more about Mr Healey, who was, at that time, front runner for the job of next leader of the Labour Party, a contest he eventually lost to become in the view of some people, perhaps the best prime minister we never had.

We met in the central lobby at Westminster, crowded with a sullen delegation from some organization like Friends of the Earth. 'It's not awfully interesting here,' Mr Healey confessed. 'Now the forces of privilege win every vote with a majority of around sixty.'

He tried to lead me through the central lobby, found we couldn't go that way during a division, and denounced the weird rules of the parliamentary bureaucrats. So we began the long walk round through Westminster Hall, out of the building and towards Mr Healey's tiny room. Before we had gone half-way he had discussed the Duke of Wellington and Harriet Wilson, the Iron Duke's girl friend, whose memoirs the former Chancellor of the Exchequer remembered started, 'It was at the age of sixteen that I became mistress to the Earl of Airlie', an autobiography which Wellington advised her, when she attempted a little blackmail, to 'Publish and be damned'.

We touched again on the ever-fascinating subject of Sir Keith Joseph, whom Mr Healey suspected might be a fundamentally decent man suffering horribly from having to propound his singularly heartless policies. The same thing, he thought, had happened to a forgotten minister named Philip Noel-Baker who was a great League of Nations man and a firm believer in peace, and then Attlee put him in charge of the Air Force, not really out of cruelty but to teach him the facts of life.

We reached his office and Mr Healey inserted himself carefully behind a small desk loaded with House of Commons writing paper. 'Well, we're not here to discuss the Duke of Wellington's mistress,' he said. 'What *are* we here for, by the way?'

I supposed we were there because of the prospect of Mr Healey eventually becoming leader of the Labour Party. He was then a man waiting to take the chance of a lifetime, poised on the brink of potential power. In all the circumstances there was little he could do or say about it, only wait, work in his Sussex garden at weekends and listen to opera when he had the opportunity.

'Will you ever be prime minister?'

'You know I can't answer questions like that. If you ask them, I shall avoid them.'

Before I encountered Mr Healey I had taken what might be called soundings, or quick chats among politicians.

'Denis must be the favourite,' said one ex-Labour MP, once one of Mr Healey's close associates. 'Provided the present method of selection stays. Of course, Jim Callaghan'll have to go first. Denis'll never run against Jim. Only Eric Heffer'll run against Jim, and he hasn't got a chance. Denis needs Jim; he needs Jim's blessing, the laying on of hands. But Jim doesn't need Denis.'

'I can't think why Jim's staying on,' said a former Cabinet Minister. 'It must be a kind of ageing vanity.'

'Does Denis get on with Jim?' I asked the one-time Labour MP.

'Listen. I once said to Denis, "What a terrible mess Jim made of things when he funked that autumn election," and Denis said,

"How could you say such a thing about the Leader? A man of profound political sense and superb judgement, a man who's never made a tactical error!" I couldn't work out if he was serious, or had his tongue in his cheek. But I tell you one thing. If he gets the job he'll be the best intellect ever to lead the Labour Party, which includes Hugh Gaitskell, so it's saying something.'

'Will they elect him?'

'If they want to win the election I think they will.'

As a matter of history, of course, they didn't.

'I was born in a bungalow in South London, during the First World War. My father was an engineer at Woolwich Arsenal,' said Mr Healey, and added with understandable pride, 'I was born on the same estate as Frankie Howerd.'

When he was five years old, Denis Healey's father became head of Keighley Technical College; the family moved to Yorkshire and the young Denis was later sent to Bradford Grammar School, which had educated Delius, the Georgian poet Humbert Wolfe, Professor Alan Bullock and would eventually receive David Hockney.

'My grandfather was an Irish Fenian. When I first stood for Parliament my father heckled me and asked me what the Labour policy was on Ireland. I had no idea. He was an Asquithian Liberal and a great admirer of Churchill. That's why my name's Denis Winston Healey. Although he was an engineer, my father was romantic and impractical. He wrote drama criticism.

'My mother was the greatest influence on me.' I remembered almost exactly the same thing having been said, in their various ways, by Mr Heath and Mr Enoch Powell. 'She was a typical H. G. Wells heroine, she had suffragette friends and I think she was a little guilty about never having been arrested. She was a teacher. I suppose you'd call us "Lower Professional Middle Class". We went to the Congregational Chapel but not too devoutly. I've been attracted by the idea of religion since then from time to time, but having lived through, and escaped from, the Communist Party I don't really want another set of ordained ideas.

'I remember seeing Eisenstein's *General Line* when I was fifteen. I was so excited by it that I wrote out the whole scenario in my notebook. There was the most wonderful discovery of montage. My heroes were the early Russian directors, Pudovkin, and Dovzhenko, who made *Earth*. Then came Hitchcock and John Huston and René Clair; I rated Jean Renoir less than his present reputation, but I was excited by Clouzot. I think Kubrick's brilliant and I'm very fond of Fellini's *Nights in Calabria*. Ken Russell, I would think, has his problems, but haven't we all?'

A new attractive vision opened of a prime minister as film director, building up the dramatic montage of events, cutting at exactly the right moment and getting some sort of a performance out of a lethargic crowd of parliamentary extras.

'I got a classical scholarship to Oxford and read Greats at Balliol. I organized a Surrealist exhibition, and introduced Oxford to Picasso's paintings of the Guernica period. It was a highly political time. Roy Jenkins was there, and Tony Crosland and Hugh Fraser, Maurice Macmillan and Ted Heath. Of course, we all knew the Second World War was coming, and quite expected not to survive. I remember Arnold Toynbee coming up and giving us a lecture in which he said, "It's the fate of your generation to be broken on the wheel, like St Catherine." All frightfully cheering stuff.'

'It was at Oxford you joined the Communist Party?'

'Oh, yes. I was in it for two years.'

Seeking to comfort Mr Healey for what will undoubtedly be thought of as an aberration, I told him of my own experiences as a one-boy Communist cell at Harrow during the early days of the war. Mr Healey heard me out with tolerance, but he didn't need to be reassured. He is totally open and honest about his undergraduate adherence to the Communist Party, which ended, naturally, in disillusion.

'The previous generation had been turned to the Labour Party by unemployment, the dole queues and the Jarrow marches. For us it was the situation in Europe, the threat of Fascism and the war in Spain, and the fight against appeasement in England which formed our political beliefs. I rememember working with Ted

Heath, who was playing astonishing organ voluntaries at Balliol, to stop the appeasement candidate, Quintin Hogg, being elected for Oxford.

'Spain was enormously important to me, to all of us, when we were young,' said Denis Healey.

At which moment someone came into the room with a tempting invitation. A trip to Madrid for Mr and Mrs Healey to take part in a television programme, everything paid for.

'I can't go, really I can't. I've got my garden party in the Leeds constituency. Edna's coming up and oh . . . what a pity!'

'It really is,' said Mr Healey when the visitor had gone. 'I'd like to have gone so much. I've never been to Spain.'

Having got a First at Oxford, Major Healey of the Royal Engineers spent the war in some danger of death; he was mentioned in dispatches, learned to live with boredom, translated Greek poetry after Sappho in north Africa, read Croce in Bari, and greatly missed his girl friend Edna, one of the five children of a crane driver from the Forest of Dean who had won the first scholarship from her school to Oxford. Mrs Healey, a lady of great intelligence and charm, recently wrote an excellent biography of Baroness Burdett-Coutts and was now engaged – and no doubt she found it a sympathetic subject – on charting the wives of those ruthless nineteenth-century Great Men, such as Dr Livingstone.

'When I came back from the war I didn't know whether to write a great work on aesthetics, take a fellowship at Merton or write the history of the Italian war.' Instead, Denis Healey became International Secretary of the Labour Party, got to know a great deal about the European Socialist movements and became MP for South-east Leeds in 1952.

'I worked a lot with Ernie Bevin and respected him enormously. He seems to me to have been like Roosevelt, a really constructive democratic politician whose aim was to build rather than destroy. I never knew Attlee so well, or Cripps. My friend Wilfred Fienburgh, who was an MP and a novelist, said talking to Attlee was like throwing biscuits to a dog.

'I didn't really get to know Nye Bevan until the end of his life;

we went to Russia together at a time when he was very conscious of his approaching death, and then I liked him very much. Before that I found him anti-American, inconsistent and not prepared to accept economic realities.

'I never understood why Hugh Gaitskell made that tremendous fuss about Clause 4 [the part of the Labour Party Constitution which committed the party to work for common ownership of the means of production, distribution and exchange]. If only he'd kept quiet about it no one would have noticed it, or even remembered it was there. I mean, can *you* remember the ten commandments?

'The Tories have changed. "Rab" Butler dragged them into the twentieth century after the war. But Mrs Thatcher has brought the party back to an unfeeling position, far from the traditions of Shaftesbury. Some of the young men in the Tory Party are more humane and I quite like Jim Prior.

'I think the turn around'll come at the end of the year, and it'll come from the number of bankruptcies in small businesses. Every Tory member will have small businessmen pleading with them and she'll have to change. The trouble is it'll be far harder to beat a Tory Party that's changed its mind. They might appear so much more attractive and reasonable.

'Is there an alternative? Of course there's an alternative. You know what I think of when Keith Joseph says, "What's the alternative . . .?" '

I sat back with eager anticipation. Sir Keith always seems to bring out the best in Mr Healey.

'. . . I think of the man who went around selling pills in the Lisbon earthquake. He kept shouting, "Pills to cure the earthquake," and someone came up and said, "You can't cure an earthquake with pills." "I know," said the old quack, "but what's your alternative?" '

'Denis? He was very tough,' said the man from the Treasury. 'But we all knew that he was very good.'

The hardline left-wing MP had said, 'Anyone but Denis for leader! He's a mini-monetarist.'

'A monetarist and water,' said the former Cabinet colleague. 'But that's better than a monetarist without water. I had a lot of time for Denis, but then, when we got the International Monetary Fund loan in 1976, he was far too obedient; although Peter Shore argued that we should follow our own policies and say to hell with the IMF, Denis wouldn't do it. And he jibed so at Tony Benn in the Cabinet. Of course, Denis is as slithery as they come in an argument. He'll say what he has to win.'

'If the Left says he's a monetarist,' said the Labour MP, 'then the Left's probably right. What would the difference be if we had a Labour Healey government instead of Thatcher? The difference would be that we'd be in and they'd be out. No, seriously. There'd be more money spent on providing jobs, which would be good to see; but there'd probably be no room for Benn in the Cabinet. It wouldn't be a radical party, as it would with Peter Shore and Benn; but, as you say, in the generally conservative with a small 'c' state of the electorate, it might win.'

'We need a mixture,' said Mr Healey. 'We need a control of the money supply and we need government intervention; we need demand management and social consensus. They have all those things in the German economy; now we've only got one. That's why we're suffering.'

'Do you think we care less about the poor than we used to?'

'Yes. It's a strange product of social equality. The nearer people are to the poor the less they sympathize with them. 'When I started in Labour politics after the war, we produced a genuine Welfare State that was thirty years ahead of any product of European Socialism. But, strangely enough, we've never learned how to manage it, or live with it, or even enjoy it. Now we've lagged behind the pragmatic Socialist parties in Europe, and the Labour Party has never really learned to live with the change it's brought about.

'When I was young I loved the "Pilgrim's Chorus" which I had on an old record. Then I got to think of Wagner as anti-semitic and dangerous. Now I love *Götterdämmerung*, but I'm nervous of my feelings about it. I like the old steadies, Bach, Beethoven and Mozart. Beethoven best, I think. Beethoven and Shakespeare.'

Middle of the road and yet highly gifted, serious but full of sharp jokes, Mr Healey, with the edge of a reputation as a bully with charm, and as the first prime minister to understand economics, film montage and Sappho, might have had a great attraction for Britain at a low ebb of self-confidence. When I met him he was sixty-two years old, ('It doesn't worry me, most of my family lived on to their nineties'), and he could only sit and wait, and avoid answering those questions nearest to his heart.

The Consolation of Byron

MICHAEL FOOT

'Here's a sigh for those who love me,
And a smile for those who hate,
And whatever sky's above me,
Here's a heart for every fate.*

Byron wrote that at a bad moment of his life, when he was forced to leave England or something, I don't know. I find it a great comfort when I read those bloody public opinion polls.'

Mr Foot had recited the verse with great enthusiasm and yet the contrast remained between the world-weary young aristocrat, accepting his destiny in a moment of lyrical bravado, and old Footie, the 69-year-old Labour leader, *Private Eye*'s Worzel Gummidge, summoning strength to face the fact that the latest poll had put his personal rating down to 14 per cent.

But, as I wrote down the verse and Mr Foot sipped whisky in what suddenly seemed a devil-may-care kind of manner, I thought that the quotation at least gave him a special place among politicians. For all I know Mr Tebbit may go through dark nights of the soul, but I doubt if he turns to Byron for company, and it seems impossible to forge any sort of link between 'Childe Harold' and, say, Mr Norman Fowler.

'I've got all 12 volumes of the new edition of Byron's letters,' said Mr Foot proudly. 'And I must say he's a great consolation.'

It was a late summer lull in the Palace of Westminster, and I sought

* Poem to Thomas Moore.

Michael Foot through a deserted Chamber and down long, unpopulated corridors. Waiting for him I peered behind a concealed door in a bookcase into the Shadow Cabinet room and saw the pictures of nineteenth-century admirals and a huge Victorian sideboard surmounted by piles of documents and a pair of high-heeled shoes. Grey-haired men in glasses, who looked like cheerful comprehensive school headmasters, began to drift out of a meeting. Denis Healey was chatting in a corridor, apparently dressed for a safari. And then Mr Foot stuck his head round a door and I was summoned into the presence.

'Of course my father was a great influence on me. He taught me how to read,' Michael Foot agreed.

'Books were his life. He was a solicitor but that was a minor occupation, just the way he got his living. He and my mother were both Methodists. Very religious. When I turned away from religion I didn't tell them. I didn't want to hurt them.'

Isaac Foot had left school at 14 but, by the time Michael was born, his had become a comfortably middle-class home. 'Did we have servants? Yes, I suppose so, from time to time. I never saw real poverty until I left Oxford during the Depression and got a job in Liverpool. I worked as a shipping clerk in a firm that belonged to the Cripps family so I got to know Stafford Cripps, who was a big influence on me.

'I was reading all the time, Shaw, Brailsford . . . I couldn't wait to get home in the evenings to read H. G. Wells. Years later Beaverbrook introduced me to H. G. Wells. He was good, but not as good as his books.

'I met Nye Bevan when I joined the Labour Party in 1934. We had years of unclouded friendship until we disagreed right at the end of his life. That was when he came out in favour of the bomb.'

I recalled that Bevan was accused of being 'a champagne socialist' – 'and you have a very comfortable house in Hampstead. Do you think a true socialist has to suffer for his beliefs?' I asked.

'Not at all, Nye always said that asceticism warps people's minds.'

'Lord Beaverbrook had a great influence on you, and you worked for his newspapers. What did you find to like about Beaverbrook?'

'I think enjoyment and a zest for life.'

I suppose it's necessary to report on Mr Foot's attire, although why the British should feel that sartorial elegance is necessary to political success I can't imagine. If Disraeli was our only dandy prime minister, Churchill achieved notable popularity by wearing an old boiler suit and a succession of eccentric hats. Suffice it to say that Mr Foot was clad in a well-pressed pair of fawn trousers, a green shirt and a tie, and his hair had been recently cut. He looks less like the scarecrow of his newspaper reputation than a pink and reasonably well-nourished don.

He speaks without the disconcerting pauses which punctuate his public orations, but his voice varies strangely in volume, so that listening to him can become like hearing someone fiddling with the wireless.

'I'd like to ask what you think about the new Conservatism', I said. 'Has the government party changed greatly?'

'I think this is the nastiest House of Commons I can remember. The mass of the Conservatives I find appalling. No breadth of vision.'

'Which Conservatives did you like?'

'I was very fond of Bob Boothby but he was really too good to be a Conservative. I think Christopher Soames is a good man. I got on very well with Randolph Churchill. I wouldn't like to ruin their political chances by giving any of the others my seal of approval, but Norman St John Stevas adds to the jollity of the place.'

'I believe you have a sneaking regard for Enoch Powell.'

'Everyone here has. It's a tragedy he made that ridiculous speech about the rivers of blood. He's by far the ablest man among them.'

'Ted Heath?'

'I suppose he has his public uses. He was savagely treated, and he can be quite brutal to *her*.'

Mr Foot gave himself another whisky with some satisfaction. 'The trouble with modern Tories is that they come from the subsidiary professions. They're PR men and chartered accountants. I do think the calibre of our members is higher.'

'You must have got to know Mrs Thatcher very well after months of prime minister's question time.'

'Who can know her? I think she's a very skilful politician. No one can deny that she's got guts, tenacity and application. But she's got no imagination, which means she's got no compassion. She's blinkered in those matters. And as for the Tebbits and so on she's created in her own image . . .'

'Do you think she's hit on some populist secret, some powerful conservative streak in the so-called "working class"?'

'I think she appeals to people's baser instincts, and to many who want to better themselves at the expense of their neighbours. She spreads that idea, and that unemployment is in some mysterious way the fault of the unemployed. A lot of people felt that in the thirties, and she's encouraged the idea to come creeping back.'

'And the Left has none of these feelings?'

'Virtue lies on the Left. I think you could say that.'

'Then the further Left you go the more virtuous you should become. But you don't find many virtues in the Militant Tendency?'

'Because they're a conspiracy against the Labour Party. They're sectarian. They call themselves Trotskyites but I think they malign Trotsky. There was a good deal to be said for Trotsky; he was far less sectarian than Stalin. They alienate people.'

'Alienate the voters?'

'Yes.'

'Do you think it's enough simply to expel Militant leaders? The Daily Express says you funked the issue.'

'I think it's enough. I think it's the fair way of doing it.'

'Would you describe yourself as a Marxist?'

'I think it's foolish to deride Marx's contribution. He was a great lover of literature, of the Bible and Shakespeare and Heine. Heine is a great hero of mine. The idea of the class war is fundamental, I think. But the hideous form that socialism has taken in Russia has been a great trauma to my generation.'

*

'You had a good life as a journalist, as a writer, you get great pleasure from books – why on earth do you want to be something like a prime minister?'

'I think once you stand for Parliament you've got to be prepared for all responsibilities. If you believe you can do a job you can't chuck your hand in.'

'Did you ever dream that getting elected leader of the Labour Party was going to be so painful?'

'Such "hard going",' Mr Foot let out a little rueful trumpet of laughter. 'No, I didn't know that. But when I had experience in government, between 1974 and 1979, I came to have more faith than ever in our policies, to believe even more strongly in a government intervening in the economy in a radical manner.'

'But did you bargain for the newspaper attacks on you, and those opinion polls we were talking about? I suppose it must be like getting bad notices.'

'Worse really. If you get bad notices at least you can take the play off. We can't. We have to keep the show on the road.'

Mr Foot gazed thoughtfully at the trophies on the bookcase, statuettes of Keir Hardie, a miner and an unknown footballer.

'Do you feel the existence of movements to get rid of you as the leader? Do you think there are plots?'

'In a party of this size there are always plots, of course. But I think I have a lot of friends, even among people who didn't support me, like Roy Hattersley. And when I go about the country I don't get a feeling that people are against me as a leader. At least they don't throw things at me.'

'But you have a few dark nights?'

'Yes.'

'And you have the consolation of Lord Byron.'

'And Hazlitt and Stendhal, and Rossini's music. And some people, of course, who are near to me.'

'Talking of Hattersley . . .'

'Did you say Hazlitt?'

'No, Hattersley . . .'

'I see. Hazlitt's better than Hattersley.'

'Didn't you write to him recently? On the subject of Dorothy Parker?'

'Oh yes. I read an article by Hattersley in which he'd attacked her works. I wrote to him and said we couldn't tolerate anyone in the Labour Party who wasn't sound on Dorothy Parker. I haven't had an answer yet so I don't know if he took me seriously.'

'You still have time to read an enormous amount, Byron, Hazlitt, Heine, Stendhal, Roy Hattersley's articles . . .'

'Oh yes. Well, you can't just read blue books, can you? It's like having straw for breakfast.'

'How are your eyes? Can you read easily?'

'One eye's gone. I had shingles, you know. But I can see perfectly well with the other. I can read all right.'

'If you were convinced that having you as a leader was really harming the Labour Party – because of your age or for any other reason – what would you do?'

'Well, I'd clear out, of course.'

'Do you think that the defectors to the SDP have betrayed you?'

'Well, yes. I've had their leaders in here – in this room where you are sitting – and begged them not to desert the party to which they owe everything. I think David Steel will see them off. He'll out-manoeuvre them, and the Liberals will get more seats than they will. I hope the SDP will fulfil its historical function by robbing votes from the Conservatives.'

'Your dream of truly democratic socialism . . . do you think it's ever worked? You've quoted Ignazio Silone who said that "the dictatorship of the proletariat enslaves socialism". Do you think we've ever had a truly just society?'

'Oddly enough I think we had one in the war. We were all united against a common enemy, and property really was being used for a common purpose.'

'Couldn't we manage that without a war?'

'They got somewhere near it in Sweden, and Austria. Norway, perhaps.'

'But it's never really been achieved?'

'No, but you've got to believe in it.'

Beginning to understand Michael Foot's sympathy with a great romantic poet, I asked: 'Can you really see it coming?'

'Nye Bevan used to say we had our "dog" periods, when we tried to live together as a group, followed by our "cat" times, when we tried to grab things for ourselves.'

'You see dog days ahead?'

'I hope so.'

'When's the next election going to be?'

'We have to be ready for it all the time, but *she* may have the arrogance to sit out her full period. People always say every election is the most important, but this must be the most vital one for Britain since the war.'

'And for the Labour Party?'

'Oh yes. Mind you, I think we'll win. Although of course we should be far ahead by now.'

'What would have been Bevan's position if he were alive now – would he be on the left or the right of the party?'

'He'd have been for unity. Nye was strongly in favour of winning elections.'

'What will happen to the Labour Party if you don't win?'

For the first time there was a silence from Mr Foot. He sat staring into space with the solemn air of a man who is once again thinking of Lord Byron:

So we'll go no more a-roving
So late into the night.

Mr Foot escorted me down flights of back stairs and a maze of passages. It seemed I was being shown out of the back entrance of the Palace of Westminster by one of its few remaining gents.

Such figures are out of fashion now that the Conservative Party has gone so resolutely and successfully down-market.

Ironically it is the Labour Party that must now try to persuade us that a fine old English gentleman with a taste for Byron might still make a humane and capable prime minister.

920
M888
Mortimer, John
In character
WITHDRAWN